T0320100

Development of the Theory of Exchange

Development of the Theory of Exchange

John Creedy

The Truby Williams Professor of Economics,
University of Melbourne, Australia

Edward Elgar

Cheltenham, UK • Northampton, MA, USA

Published by
Edward Elgar Publishing Limited
Glensanda House
Montpellier Parade
Cheltenham
Glos GL50 1UA
UK

Edward Elgar Publishing, Inc.
6 Market Street
Northampton
Massachusetts 01060
USA

A catalogue record for this book
is available from the British Library

Library of Congress Cataloguing in Publication Data

Creedy, John, 1949-
    Development of the theory of exchange / John Creedy.
    Includes bibliographical references and index.
    1. Commerce. 2. Exchange. 3. Demand (Economic theory)
4. Economics. I. Title.
HF1008.C73   1999
380.1–dc21   98–31082
                                                     CIP

ISBN 1 85898 920 5

Printed and bound in Great Britain by
Biddles Ltd, Guildford and King's Lynn

Contents

III   Selections from the Texts

List of Figures

List of Tables

Part I

Introduction

Chapter 1

Introduction and Outline

The aim of this book is to provide an outline of the development of the theory of exchange, with an emphasis on the formal models produced during roughly the last half of the 19th century. This is achieved in two ways. First, part II provides an introductory survey of the developement of the theory. Secondly, on the grounds that there is no substitute for reading the work of the pioneers, part III reproduces extracts from some of their major contributions.

Several different threads in the development of exchange models can be distinguished. There is the French contribution involving Cournot's analysis of trade between regions, which was later extended by Walras into a complete model of exchange with a utility maximising foundation. Over a similar period, there was the work in England stemming from J.S. Mill's treatment of international trade, which stimulated the analyses of Whewell and then Marshall, each of which involved a non-utility framework. These developments in France and England were more or less independent except that Marshall, following serious study of Cournot's model, deliberately rejected his approach (despite the strong influence on other aspects of Marshall's work) in favour of that of Mill.

A further thread involves the pioneering contribution of Jevons, whose work was first carried out during his time spent in Australia, and his utility maximising approach. Jevons was in turn the major influence on Edgeworth, who effectively provided the 'grand synthesis' of the approaches of the various writers mentioned, as well as producing his own extremely important innovations. Following this, in a period that may be described as the high point in the cosmopolitan development of economics, Launhardt in Germany and Wicksell in Sweden provided masterly expositions of the work of other writers in addition to making their original contributions. In particular, Launhardt explored in great detail what is now referred to as the welfare economics of the model. It would of course be possible to add many more names to the list of those contributing to the developement of the modern theory of exchange, but this book concentrates on these seminal contributions.

When these various threads in the literature are pulled together, what emerges is the view that the various models have many formal similarities. However, this analytical similarity is often disguised by the different approaches used and the different stresses placed on various aspects of the model by the various writers.

The following section of this chapter emphasises the central role of exchange in the work of the early neoclassical economists. This role appears often to have been neglected in much of the more modern secondary literature on the period. The final section of this chapter provides a brief outline of the book.

1.1   The Central Role of Exchange

A distinguishing feature of the economic analysis of roughly the last third of the 19th century was its emphasis on exchange as the central economic problem. Hicks, following Edgeworth, referred to the early neoclassicals as 'catallactists' in order to emphasise the exchange focus. He stressed that, 'while the classics looked at the economic system primarily from the production angle, the catallactists looked at it primarily from the side of exchange. It was possible, they found, to construct a "vision" of economic life out of the theory of exchange, as the classics had done out of the social product. It was quite a different vision' (1984, p.250). Edgeworth (1925, ii, p.288) summarised the position by suggesting that, 'in pure economics there is only one fundamental theorem, but that is a very difficult one: the theory of bargain in a wide sense'.

A similar point was made by Schumpeter (1954, p.911) who wrote of the neoclassical economists that, 'they realised the central position of exchange value' which 'is but a special form of a universal coefficient of transformation on the derivation of which pivots the whole logic of economic phenomena'. In considering the central position of exchange theory, Fraser (1937, p.104) stated that the view of costs in terms of foregone alternatives is 'merely the extension of the exchange relationship to the whole of economic life'.

There are two primary ingredients of an exchange analysis. The first is an appreciation of the principle of reciprocal demand and supply while the second is the concept of demand as a function of relative prices. Early examples of treatments of exchange, including Aristotle, Beccaria, Courcelle-Seneuil, Turgot, Cantillon, Canard, Isnard and Verri, show how little real progress can be made without these two elements combined, despite the useful insights provided; on the early writers, see Theocharis (1961). However, the neoclassical economists were not the first to recognise these requirements or attempt to construct a model of exchange based on them. International trade provided an important context in which exchange theories were considered; prime examples considered in this book include Cournot, J.S. Mill and Whewell. As Edgeworth stressed, 'the fundamental principle of international trade is that general theory which Jevons called the Theory of Exchange ... which constitutes the "kernel" of most of the chief problems of economics' (1925, ii, p.6). He added, 'distribution is the species of exchange by which produce is divided between the parties who have contributed to it' (1925, ii, p.13).

The great analytical success of the early neoclassical economists was also associated with the fact that they provided a foundation for their exchange model in the form of a utility analysis. This allowed for a deeper treatment of the gains from exchange and the wider consideration of economic welfare. Furthermore, this type of welfare analysis survived the replacement of a cardinal utility concept with an ordinal concept, or the idea of a simple preference ordering. Indeed, Hicks suggested that 'welfare economics was captured by the catallactists and it has never got quite free' (1984, p.253).

In his discussion of the work of the early neoclassical writers, Hicks (1984, p.252) expressed the view that 'the principal reason for the triumph of catallactics – in its day it was quite a triumph – was nothing to do with socialism or individualism; nor did it even have much to do with the changes that were then occurring in the "real world". The construction of a powerful economic theory, based on exchange, instead of production and distribution, had always been a possibility. The novelty in the work of the great catallactists is just that they achieved it.' This strongly expressed view may not find favour among modern 'relativists' and those who attach great importance to the sociology of knowledge, but it is nevertheless a persuasive argument.

It is only when the perceived central position of exchange analysis is recognised, along with the place of the principle of utility maximisation as the foundation, that it is possible to have some appreciation of the attitude behind Edgeworth's (1881, p.12) remark, following a discussion of the extension of utility analysis to subjects such as production and labour supply, that '"Mécanique Sociale" may one day take her place along with "Mécanique Celeste", throned each upon the double-sided height of one maximum principle, the supreme pinnacle of moral as of physical science ... the movements of each soul, whether selfishly isolated or linked sympathetically, may continually be realising the maximum energy of pleasure, the Divine love of the universe'. Of course, other writers were much more prosaic in their expressions than Edgeworth, but his view nicely encapsulates something of the pioneering spirit of the early neoclassical economists. A further example of this enthusiasm can be found in Jevons's letter to his sister, reproduced in Black (1977, ii, pp.361, 410). Schumpeter argued that the utility analysis must be understood in the context of exchange as the central 'pivot', and 'the whole of the organism of pure economics thus finds itself unified in the light of a single principle – in a sense in which it never had before' (1954, p.913).

The central role of exchange is unfortunately seldom stressed in modern texts or histories of economic analysis, where emphasis is placed on the idea of a 'marginal revolution' associated with the concept of marginal utility, which of course arises naturally from the first-derivatives needed in a utility maximising approach. The idea of the margin has, however, a much longer history in economics. But the emphasis is such that priority of place is often given to the adjective rather than the noun (in marginal utility), with stress on the introduction of calculus methods, or at least notation.[1] The context of discussions is typically the derivation of partial equilibrium demand curves, even though such curves hardly ever appeared in the early major works of Jevons, Walras, Edgeworth, Wicksell or even Marshall. It is suggested that this view of the neoclassicals is not helpful and actually creates something of a barrier to reaching an understanding of their approach. Indeed, Hicks (1984, p.250) suggested that the term marginal revolution 'is a bad term, for it misses the essence of what was involved'.

1.2 Outline of the Book

Part II of this book aims to provide a review of the major developments in the theory of exchange. Rather than taking a purely chronological approach, the discussion is divided into two chapters, dealing respectively with non-utility approaches and the introduction of a utility foundation. In what follows, reference is generally made to the available source; in Cournot's case the Bacon translation edited by Fisher, rather than the original date of publication. Chapter 2 begins the examination of non-utility approaches to exchange with Cournot's (1927) model of trade between two regions, involving a single good and dating from 1838. Both Walras and Marshall rejected this approach and recognised that it could not be extended simply by adding more demand and supply equations; the fundamental concept of reciprocal demand and supply has to be at the heart of any exchange model. As shown in section 2.2, Walras took the most direct route while Marshall took Mill as his starting point. Mill's analysis, along with the mathematical model produced by Whewell, is discussed in section 2.3. Marshall's extension, using offer curves, is considered in section 2.4. An important lesson, as suggested above, is that Walras and Marshall produced a model with many formal similarities, leading to their emphasis on multiple equilibria and stability issues, but used different

---

[1]The famous remark regarding adjective and noun is from Hutchison (1953).

diagrammatic approaches that are directly and simply linked. Indeed, reference may be made to a Mill/Whewell/Walras/Marshall model. However, they stressed different aspects of the model, so that the initial appearance is very different and the origins are not obvious.

Chapter 3 turns to the utility maximising foundations of exchange, starting in section 3.1 with the pioneering contribution of Jevons. Section 3.2 then examines Walras's approach, paying particular attention to the differing attitudes of the two writers to the same fundamental 'equations of exchange'. Both Jevons and Walras concentrated on price-taking solutions to these equations. Some commentators would dispute this point, placing much stress on different interpretations of Walras's famous *tâtonnement* process. But in the formal models it is hard to escape the fact that in both Walras's and Jevons's approach, individuals are price-takers and that, in the equilibria considered, all exchange takes place at the corresponding prices; trading at disequilibrium prices is considered in section 3.4 below. In examining price-taking, Jevons left the equations in terms of quantities exchanged, with the equilibrium price ratio to be determined by the resulting ratio of quantities exchanged. Walras instead introduced the price at an early stage and thereby showed the route by which the general equilibrium demand and supply curves that he had produced in extending Cournot's model can be derived. Section 3.3 then briefly discusses Edgeworth's treatment of exchange, representing the high point in the development of formal exchange models.

Section 3.4 discusses two closely related contributions to the literature, by Launhardt (1993) and Wicksell (1954), dating from 1885 and 1893 respectively. These can in many ways be regarded as masterly expositions of the theory, despite their lack of familiarity with Edgeworth's *Mathematical Psychics,* which would have been difficult to obtain. However, Launhardt made a number of original extensions of his own: indeed, it can be argued that his book represents the first major treatise on welfare economics. These contributions warrant closer analysis in view of the fact that, like Walras, they were not translated into English for many years. Furthermore, Launhardt's reputation was damaged by unfair criticisms by Wicksell, as discussed below, who nevertheless relied heavily on the former's work.

As already indicated, part III provides extracts from some of the major, or classic, contributions to the theory of exchange. As suggested above, these selections obviously exclude many important works in the area; they have been chosen mainly in order to link reasonably closely with the material in part II. However, a different organisation of the material has been adopted instead of the the largely non-chronological approach used when reviewing the theory. Given the importance of the concept of the demand curve as a functional relationship, it is useful to begin, in chapter 4, with discussions of demand by Cournot and Whewell. Cournot examines the variation in total revenue with price, and comes close to defining an elasticity concept, while Whewell makes the basic elasticity idea the central focus of his treatment of demand and thereby restricts his treatment to small changes in prices. Chapter 5 presents selections from the international trade models of Cournot, J.S. Mill and Whewell. Chapter 6 concentrates on the formal exchange models of Jevons and Walras, although it begins with earlier discussions of exchange by Cantillon, Turgot and Hearn, which provide an interesting contrast. The selection of material from Walras actually presented the greatest difficulty in view of his prolixity; the extracts given here provide little more than a flavour of what Edgeworth (1889, p.435) called 'the exuberance of algebraic foliage'.[2] Marshall and Edgeworth are represented in chapter 7, while chapter 8 provides extracts from the later closely related expositions of the theory of exchange by Launhardt and Wicksell.

In presenting extracts from some of these classic works on exchange, a decision was made to avoid providing any kind of editorial material, particularly in view of the discussion provided in part II. Where material has been omitted, this is simply marked by ellipses (...) with no indication of whether just a few words or several paragraphs have been left out. A substantial number of the original footnotes and cross-references have been silently omitted. In some works, the paragraph numbers have also been excluded and, where relevant, the punctuation has been removed from the mathematical equations. Instead of using the original numbering for equations and

---

[2]Edgeworth complained in the same review that Walras 'diffuses over some thirty-five pages an idea which might have been adequately presented in a few paragraphs'.

figures, they have been given numbers appropriate for the chapter in which they are included, although equation numbers are given only if they appear in the original.[3] The quotation marks have been removed from the material in Mill's chapter on international trade, where he reproduced material from earlier work. Titles have been given to the figures, although in all cases the originals contained no titles. Corrections have been silently made in the material from Edgeworth's *Mathematical Psychics,* though further details can be found in Creedy (1986a).

This approach will obviously offend scholars (it is sincerely hoped there are some scholars left to be offended); but given the aim of this book, to concentrate on the development of the formal analysis of exchange models, this approach was judged to be appropriate. The original material is included to support the earlier discussion and to provide a stimulus to further reading, not to provide source material to be used for purposes of exegesis. Very brief introductions are given in italics to distinguish them from the texts reproduced; in most cases further discussion and references can be obtained from the material contained in part II.

---

[3]This decision regarding numbering was dictated mainly by the constraints imposed by the word processor used to produce the camera ready copy.

Part II

Development of the Theory

Chapter 2

Non-utility Approaches

This chapter examines the development of non-utility approaches to the analysis of exchange. It begins in section 2.1 with Cournot's (1927) attempt to examine trade in a single good, involving two regions. On this analysis Edgeworth later commented, not without sympathy, that 'the lesson of caution in dealing with a subject and method so difficult is taught by no example more impressively than by that of Cournot. This superior intelligence ... seems not only to have slipped at several steps, but even to have taken a wholly wrong direction' (1925, ii, p.47). Its importance lies in the fact that Cournot's model provided an influential starting point for the development of a general equilibrium approach.

A major value of Cournot's work in this area seems to have been the stimulus it provided to Walras and Marshall to attempt to improve the basic model. Walras's extension is examined in section 2.2. There is quite separate English development of a non-utility analysis in the work of J.S. Mill, which stimulated the work by Whewell on a formal statement of Mill's model; these contributions are examined in section 2.3. It is indeed Mill, rather than Cournot, who provides the link to Marshall; this is discussed in section 2.4. Despite the somewhat different line of development and the different emphasis placed on aspects of their analysis, Marsall and Walras can nevertheless be seen to have been working with essentially the same formal model.

The formal similarity of the basic models used by Walras and Marshall, who both stressed multiple equilibria and examined stability properties, has not always been recognised. For example, some economists, including Jaffé (in Walras, 1954, p.504) have argued strongly that the approaches were different. However, the 'substantially equivalent' nature of the two analyses was stressed by Hicks, who suggested that 'one feels almost obliged to explain it by the intrinsic excellence of the path they followed. Yet in fact there is a clear historical reason for it, one decisive influence we know to have been felt by both. Each of them had read Cournot' (1934, p.346). Hicks's statement must, however, be qualified by the recognition that while Walras explicitly extended Cournot, Marshall (after rejecting Cournot's approach) extended Mill's treatment which itself provided such an impressive use of the basic ingredients of an exchange model and was produced almost ten years before that of Cournot. It does indeed seem that 'intrinsic excellence' played a major role.

2.1   Cournot's Trade Model

2.1.1   The Basic Framework

Cournot's (1838, translated 1927) framework was one in which a single good is initially produced in two countries that are isolated from each other. When 'communication' between the markets occurs, the good is produced and exported by the country in which it is initially cheaper, allowing for transport costs. The market demand and supply curves were taken as given, and the regions have a common currency. In isolation the equilibrium price of the good is p_a and p_b in markets A and B respectively, with demand functions $F_a(p)$ and $F_b(p)$, and supply functions $\Omega_a(p)$ and $\Omega_b(p)$. The prices are given by the intersecting partial equilibrium curves and are the solutions to:

$$\Omega_a(p_a) = F_a(p_a) \tag{2.1}$$

and

$$\Omega_b(p_b) = F_b(p_b) \tag{2.2}$$

If $p_a < p_b$ and the difference exceeds the cost of transporting the good between the two markets, ε, then the good is exported from A to B. Cournot argued that trade equalises the price of the good in the two markets, except for the transport costs. If the new equilibrium price in market A is denoted p'_a, Cournot (1927, p.119) stated that this is given as the solution to:

$$\Omega_a(p'_a) + \Omega_b(p'_a + \varepsilon) = F_a(p'_a) + F_b(p'_a + \varepsilon) \tag{2.3}$$

so that total supply is equal to total demand in both markets combined. Cournot wrote:

$$p'_a = p_a + \delta \text{ and } p_b = p_a + \omega \tag{2.4}$$

so that δ is the change in the price in market A and ω is the pre-trade absolute difference between prices in the two markets. Trade takes place only if $\omega > \varepsilon$. Substitute for $p_a = p_b - \omega$ in the first of the expressions in (2.4) and add ε to get:

$$p'_a + \varepsilon = p_b + \delta + \varepsilon - \omega \tag{2.5}$$

Equation (2.3) can then be re-written as:

$$\Omega_a(p_a + \delta) + \Omega_b(p_b + \delta + \varepsilon - \omega) = F_a(p_a + \delta) + F_b(p_b + \delta + \varepsilon - \omega) \tag{2.6}$$

This expression can be simplified using Cournot's method of 'development and reduction' which involves taking the Taylor series expansion of each function of the form $F(p + \delta)$ and neglecting squares and higher powers of δ. Thus:

$$F(p + \delta) = F(p) + \delta F'(p) \tag{2.7}$$

Expanding each term in (2.6) in this way, and using (2.1) and (2.2), Cournot (1927, p.120) obtained:

$$\delta\{\Omega'_a(p_a) - F'_a(p_a)\} = (\delta + \varepsilon - \omega)\{F'_b(p_b) - \Omega'_b(p_b)\} \tag{2.8}$$

Demand curves are assumed to slope downwards and supply curves to slope upwards, so the term in curly brackets on the left hand side of (2.8) is positive, while that on the right hand side is negative. Since $\delta > 0$, then $\delta + \varepsilon - \omega < 0$ and $\delta < \varepsilon$. Hence the increase in price in market A must be less than the difference between the initial price differential and the unit transport cost.

Cournot used this model to examine the gains from trade using the concepts of consumer and producer surplus, and investigated the conditions under which the total demand in the two markets combined would increase. This can be shown to depend on the ratio of demand to supply elasticities in each country, though of course Cournot did not use the concept of elasticity himself; for further details, see Creedy (1992b; 1992c, pp.29-31). Cournot's discussion of the basic concept of the demand curve and his investigation of the condition under which total revenue is maximised, where he came very close to the elasticity concept, is reproduced in chapter 4 below.

He also considered the question of whether the value of output would increase. In examining import or export taxes, Cournot made an algebraic slip which led him to believe that the price may fall in the importing country, although in fact price must rise in the importing, and fall in the exporting, country. This was briefly discussed by Edgeworth (1894, reprinted in 1925, ii, p.49), where he noted that Berry and Sanger, two former pupils of Marshall, had independently made the correction. The error was later also pointed out by Fisher, in Cournot (1927, p.xxiv). A selection from Cournot's treatment of trade between regions is given in chapter 5.

2.1.2   A Diagrammatic Version

Marshall (1975, ii, pp.246-248) made an early attempt to cast Cournot's model into diagrammatic form, mainly for the purpose of examining the gains from trade using measures of producers' and consumers' surplus. The diagrammatic analysis of the model was later refined by Marshall's student Cunynghame (1892, 1903). He suggested that 'the method of treating economics graphically is probably due to Cournot' and added, 'the chief credit of reviving an interest in this method rests with Professor Marshall' (1892, p.36). This work culminated in Cunynghame's book (1904), reviewed at length by Edgeworth (1905). It does not seem to be widely recognised that Cunynghame's treatment stems directly from Cournot. Viner (1955, p.589), the major historian of international trade theory, referred to Barone's use of the same diagram to measure the gains from trade, but did not seem to recognise that the diagram represents Cournot's model.[1]

---

[1]The origins were, however, recognised by Samuelson (1952).

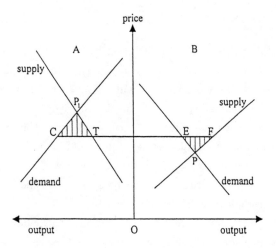

Figure 2.1: Cournot's Trade Model

After an unsatisfactory start (1892, p.44), Cunynghame produced a 'back-to-back' diagram without any reference to Cournot but virtually paraphrasing the latter's introduction to his model (1903, p.317). Ignoring transport costs, the diagram is shown in Figure 2.1 where the equilibrium price is such that $CT = EF$. Marshall's notes show the influence of Cournot on Marshall's analysis of consumers' and producers' surplus. Marshall's diagrams translate Cournot's surplus analysis into the now familiar triangles. Using the back-to-back version of Figure 2.1, the left hand side shows that the gain to B's consumers arising from the price reduction outweighs the loss to producers, so that the net gain is equal to the shaded area P_1CT. The price increase in A produces a net gain equal to the shaded area EPF in the right hand side of the figure. Marshall added that if in each country the cost of production is independent of output, then the exporting country gains nothing from trade (1975, ii, pp.247-248). Although these notes are not dated, there seems little doubt that Cournot was the sole influence and that Jenkin's (1871) analysis was quite independent, as Marshall himself always insisted.

2.2   Walras's Extension

A fundamental criticism of Cournot's model is that it deals with only one
good. This point was acknowledged by Cournot towards the end of the
Researches, where he wrote that 'It will be said that it is impossible for
exportation of a commodity to fail to involve importation on the exporting
market of a precisely equal value; and reciprocally, importation on a market
involves exportation of an equal value ... It would be necessary to consider
each of these nations as acting simultaneously the part of an importing nation
and that an exporting nation, which would greatly complicate the question
and lead to a complex result' (1927, pp.161-162).

It was left to Walras to make the extension. This cannot be achieved
simply by adding another good and imposing a balance of payments constraint. Additional partial equilibrium demand and supply curves cannot
by their very nature cope with the interdependence which is at the heart of
the problem. Walras's autobiography states that he 'soon perceived' that
Cournot's approach could not be applied to exchange and, 'restricting my
attention, therefore, to the case of two commodities, I rationally derived
from the demand curve of each commodity the supply curve of the other and
demonstrated how current equilibrium results from the intersection of the
supply and demand curves' (quoted in Jaffé, 1983, p.25). Walras's transformation of Cournot's model, using the same notation, is contained in Walras
(1954, pp.81-114). The crucial ingredient is the recognition that 'to say that
a quantity D_a of (A) is demanded at the price p_a is, *ipso facto*, the same
thing as saying that a quantity O_b of (B), equal to $D_a p_a$, is being offered'
(1954, p.88).

Jaffé (1983, pp.55-77) argued that the line of filiation is instead from Isnard to Walras. Isnard recognised the important point that the price ratio is
equivalent to the (inverse) ratio of quantities exchanged. He also addressed
the mutual interdependence in a general equilibrium system. But his discussion was restricted merely to given quantities; there is no analysis of demand
as a function of relative prices. A section from Isnard's analysis is reproduced
in Baumol and Goldfeld (1968, pp.255-257), who suggest that strong claims

made for him are 'somewhat over-enthusiastic' (1968, p.253).

Suppose that there are two goods, X and Y, and comparative advantage is such that country A exports good X to country B, while the latter exports good Y to A. Assume complete specialisation, and denote the relative price of good X as p. This relative price can be interpreted as the amount of good Y that must be given in order to obtain a unit of good X. For present purposes it is necessary to express B's demand for X and A's demand for Y as $F_b(p)$ and $F_a(p^{-1})$ respectively; p^{-1} is the relative price of Y. The essential feature of an exchange model is that the demand for one good, at a given price, automatically carries with it a supply of the other good. B's supply of Y, corresponding to the demand $F_b(p)$, is thus given by:

$$\Omega_b(p) = pF_b(p) \qquad (2.9)$$

while A's supply of X is given by:

$$\Omega_a(p) = p^{-1}F_a\left(p^{-1}\right) \qquad (2.10)$$

The equilibrium price is that value of p for which the demand for and supply of, say, Y, are equal. This requires:

$$\Omega_b(p) = pF_b(p) = F_a\left(p^{-1}\right) \qquad (2.11)$$

which is equivalent to the equilibrium condition for good X, given by:

$$\Omega_a(p) = p^{-1}F_a\left(p^{-1}\right) = F_b(p) \qquad (2.12)$$

The general equilibrium model therefore requires only the specification of the two demand functions in terms of the relative price, p; the associated supply curves are obtained using the reciprocal demand relationship. It was this insight that later led Wicksteed (1933) to argue that the concept of the partial equilibrium supply curve is 'profoundly misleading' and should be abandoned altogether. Wicksteed emphasised the role of endowments, or stocks, but surprisingly he did not use the apparatus of Walras and Jevons with which he was so familiar; see Creedy (1991a).

The fact that B's supply curve is given by $pF_b(p)$ shows that it behaves in the same way as the total revenue, when $F_b(p)$ is regarded as being a partial equilibrium demand curve and p is simply the price, rather than the relative price, as here. This is of course the problem examined by Cournot, mentioned above, and in the extract given in chapter 4 below. Walras's extension of Cournot's model is contained in the material given in chapter 6 below.

2.2.1   Linear Demands

In order to explore the nature of the model, suppose that these functions are linear, such that:

$$F_b\left(p\right) = a - bp \tag{2.13}$$

and

$$F_a\left(p^{-1}\right) = \alpha - \beta p^{-1} \tag{2.14}$$

From A's demand for Y in (2.14), the corresponding supply of X is obtained using (2.10) as:

$$\Omega_a\left(p\right) = \alpha p^{-1} - \beta p^{-2} \tag{2.15}$$

and equilibrium price is that which equates (2.15) and (2.13), giving:

$$\beta - \alpha p + ap^2 - bp^3 = 0 \tag{2.16}$$

so that three equilibria, not necessarily real or distinct, exist. This approach therefore rapidly gives rise to the need to consider the stability of alternative equilibrium positions. The comparative static properties of models with multiple equilibria are of much interest, since small changes in demand conditions can lead to a large jump in the equilibrium price. The supply curve of X is 'backward bending' (if p is on the vertical axis), with supply reaching a maximum when $p = 2\beta/\alpha$ and a point of inflection where $p = 3\beta/\alpha$. Furthermore the maximum supply, where the price elasticity of supply is zero, occurs at a price for which the elasticity of demand (for Y) is minus one. It is the backward bending property that gives rise to the possibility of three equilibria. On the equilibrium properties of this model and its implications for the distribution of prices, see Creedy and Martin (1993, 1994).

The diagrammatic representation of this model, using a simple modification of Figure 2.1, is shown in Figure 2.2. The analysis may be extended by

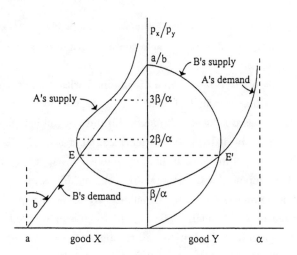

Figure 2.2: Exchange with Linear Demands

using (2.13) to write $p = \{a - F_b(p)\}/b$. Substituting this expression for p into equation (2.9) gives:

$$\Omega_b(p) = F_b(p)\{a - F_b(p)\}/b \qquad (2.17)$$

Equation (2.17) has a simple interpretation as the 'offer curve' of country B, the concept introduced by Marshall. This offer curve is quadratic, so that if both countries have linear demand curves, the offer curves may intersect three times, consistent with the result from (2.16). It is well known that the turning point of an offer curve occurs at the point of unit demand elasticity, which is precisely the same condition under which Walras's supply curve turns backwards; on the diagrammatic link between the two frameworks, see Creedy (1990a; 1992c, pp.94-96).

2.3   The Mill–Whewell Model

The previous subsection considered the path taken from Cournot to Walras. However, the same exchange model has a quite separate line of development, running from J.S. Mill and Whewell to Marshall. Walras did not appear to be influenced by Mill's trade model, despite his familiarity with Mill's work. His published correspondence suggests that he did not become aware of Whewell's model until after he made contact with Jevons; see Jaffé (1965, I, letters 328, 375).

The concept of reciprocal demand combined with the clear idea of demand as a schedule was in fact explored by Mill almost a decade before Cournot's book was published, although Mill did not publish his analysis of international trade until 1844. A mathematical analysis of Mill's model was produced by Whewell in 1850. In his first published paper, Marshall (1876) indicated his preference for the general approach of Mill rather than Cournot, and his offer curves were directly stimulated by Mill's analysis. Ironically, the precise nature of Marshall's offer curves was misunderstood by Cunynghame, who went so far as to criticise Marshall's analysis on the grounds that it should deal explicitly with more demand and supply curves (1903, p.317). Marshall commented rather tersely in a letter to Cunynghame that, 'as to international trade curves – mine were set to a definite tune, that called by Mill' (in Pigou, 1925, p.451).

2.3.1   Mill's 'Great Chapter'

In considering the determination of the terms of trade between the comparative cost ratios of two countries, Mill was able to indicate the importance of reciprocal demand much more clearly than previous writers because of his conception of demand as a schedule; see, for example, (1920, p.585). Mill's conception of demand in terms of a schedule is stressed by Robbins (1958, p.242) when comparing his trade analysis with that of Torrens, and by O'Brien (1975, p.183). Despite the importance of Torrens's and Pennington's work in international trade, Viner (1955, p.447) stresses the pivotal role of Mill's analysis for subsequent work. Although Pennington refers to the strength of demand when examining the gains from trade, he suggests (1840, pp.36, 39, 40-41) that the exchange rate will fluctuate between extremes, rather than tend to some determinate value. The high quality of Joplin's work in this area, neglected for many years, is now clear from O'Brien (1993, pp.211-219).

Mill did not use mathematical notation, preferring to give numerical examples. The crucial element of the analysis is the idea that demand depends on relative prices. Hence England, assumed to have a comparative advantage over Germany in the production of cloth (while Germany has a comparative advantage in linen production), has a demand for linen that depends on its price relative to that of cloth. This relative price can be expressed in terms of an amount of cloth per unit of linen. This is the basis of Mill's argument that 'all trade is in reality barter, money being a mere instrument for exchanging things' (1920, p.583).

If England demands a certain quantity of linen, there is an associated, or reciprocal, supply of cloth equal to the amount of linen multiplied by the relative price. The quantity of linen multiplied by the amount of cloth per unit of linen obviously gives an amount of cloth. Neglecting transport costs, equilibrium requires that the post-trade relative price is the same in each country and that the price is such that Germany's import demand for cloth precisely matches England's export supply (associated with its demand for linen at the corresponding relative price). After giving a numerical example, Mill added that, 'as the inclinations and circumstances of consumers cannot be reduced to any rule, so neither can the proportions in which the two commodities will be interchanged' (1920, p.587).

He then went on, when considering the gains from trade, to add that 'the circumstances on which the proportionate share of each country more remotely depends, admit only of a very general indication' (1920, p.587). It is in Mill's subsequent discussion of such 'general indications' that he used the concept of demand elasticity – although he described it with the term 'susceptibility'. Mill effectively argued (1920, p.587-588) that if the German demand for cloth is completely inelastic, then all the gains from trade go to Germany. In general, Mill was able to demonstrate that 'If, therefore, it be asked what country draws to itself the greatest share of the advantage of any trade it carries on, the answer is, the country for whose production there is in other countries the greatest demand, and a demand the most susceptible of increase from additional cheapness' (1920, p.591). Mill also introduced additional countries, transport costs, and additional goods, as well as examining the effects of technological change and shifts in demand; for further discussion of Mill and his critics, see Creedy (1990a).

Part of Mill's chapter on international trade is reproduced in chapter 5 below.

2.3.2   Whewell's Mathematical Model

Whewell (1850) produced a mathematical version of Mill's analysis, suggesting that the use of numerical examples led to the neglect of several important factors. Whewell denoted the English demand for linen and its relative price before trade as q and p respectively, with the German demand for cloth and its pre-trade relative price as Q and P respectively. After-trade prices and quantities are distinguished by the use of a dash, so that the equality of prices means that: means that:

$$p'P' = 1 \qquad (2.18)$$

(since, for example, P' is the reciprocal of the price of linen relative to that of cloth in Germany). The reciprocal supply of cloth implied by England's demand for linen is, from the earlier argument, simply $p'q'$. Hence trade balance is achieved when:

$$p'q' = Q' \qquad (2.19)$$

As a result of trade, the relative price of linen in England and that of cloth in Germany would fall by proportions x and X respectively, so that:

$$p' = p\,(1 - x) \ \text{ and } \ P' = P\,(1 - X) \qquad (2.20)$$

If, in addition, the relative price of linen in Germany before trade is a proportion, k, lower than in England, then $1/P = p(1 - k)$, and combining this with (2.20) and (2.18) gives:

$$X = \frac{k - x}{1 - x} \qquad (2.21)$$

A feature of Whewell's model is his treatment of demand. He supposed that, for the English linen demand, the proportionate fall in the relative price, of x, would lead to a proportionate fall in 'revenue' (which in this context is the reciprocal supply of cloth) of mx. The coefficient m was referred to as the 'specific rate of change' of the commodity, which Whewell supposed would vary over the demand curve. In fact it is possible to show that m is simply one plus the elasticity of demand; for further analysis see Creedy (1989). Similarly M is the 'specific rate of change' of the German demand for cloth. Hence:

$$p'q' = pq\,(1 - mx) \text{ and } P'Q' = PQ\,(1 - MX) \tag{2.22}$$

Substituting (2.21) and (2.22) into (2.19) gives, after rearranging, Whewell's result that:

$$x = \frac{n\,(1 - Mk) - 1}{n\,(1 - M) - m} \tag{2.23}$$

where $n = PQ/q$ and is the value of cloth demanded in Germany before trade divided by the value of linen consumed in England before trade, measured in German prices. Alternatively n can be interpreted as the German pre-trade opportunity cost of cloth in terms of linen foregone, divided by the English demand for linen before trade. Whewell argued that when $x = 0$, England gains all the advantage from trade, and when $x = k$ (that is, when $X = 0$), Germany obtains all the advantage. It is therefore possible to obtain the limiting values of n under which trade takes place. Whewell's result gives a precise expression from which the terms of trade can be obtained in terms of the two demand elasticities and the relative 'sizes' of the two countries as measured by their demand. He also indicated that a country which receives no advantage from trade may well not specialise; that is, part of its relatively large demand for the imported good will be met from domestic production.

Whewell therefore made a significant advance over Mill's analysis. The main limitation of his approach is the highly restrictive specification of demand, which is strictly limited to small price changes. It is argued that Whewell's results provided the major impetus for Mill's supplementary sections, added in a later edition. Although Mill (1920, p.586) only mentioned Thornton, he had other 'intelligent criticism' in mind. Thornton may well have argued that the type of 'equilibrium' indicated by Mill might not be unique, a point Mill acknowledged at the beginning of the supplementary sections. Thornton's emphasis on indeterminacy in barter was also noted by

Jevons and Edgeworth; see Creedy (1986a, p.48).

Mill's concern with multiple equilibria might have been reinforced by the recognition, indicated by Whewell, that m and M would generally vary along the respective demand curves. Mill's attempt to deal with non-uniqueness is of interest. However, there is much stronger contextual evidence that Mill's discussion of the limits within which his 'equation' applied, his recognition of partial specialisation and emphasis on the domestic transfer of resources came directly from Whewell; see in particular Mill (1920, p.598). Mill's discussion of inelastic, unitary, and elastic demands can easily be generated by appropriate substitution into (2.23) above. Chipman (1965) interpreted Mill as assuming constant unit elasticities of demand, but this is strongly criticised by Appleyard and Ingram (1979); on this issue, see also Creedy (1992c, pp.97-100) and on stability analysis, see Amano (1968).

In its essential components, Whewell's mathematical model of Mill is precisely the same as Walras's later generalisation of Cournot's one-good model. He specified only the two demand curves required, and used the concept of reciprocal demand and supply to generate the supply curves. The translation of Whewell's model into diagrammatic form gives the same type of diagram as that shown in Figure 2.2 above.[2] The major difference is that the detail of Whewell's model was more cumbersome, because of his awkward specification of the functional relationship between price and quantity changes. It meant that he arrived at an early formal statement of the concept of price elasticity, of which he made good use, but the simple specification used by Walras, modified from Cournot, was much more powerful. Whewell's treatment led to a certain amount of difficulty for later commentators; see Creedy (1989; 1992c, pp.24-28).

Whewell's treatment of the demand curve was in fact first produced by him in 1829 in the context of his criticism of Ricardo. A selection from his later discussion is contained in chapter 4 below. Mention may be made here of the fact that, in discussing the specification of demand curves, Whewell

---

[2]This was in fact the path taken by the present writer, in trying to see the link in diagrammatic terms between Mill and Marshall, without realising that the same diagram (or half of it) was in Walras.

was the first to notice that the famous King–Davenant 'law of demand' precisely follows a cubic; see Creedy (1986b). Part of Whewell's 1850 paper on international trade is given in chapter 5 below.

2.4 From Mill to Marshall

It has been suggested that the diagrammatic form of Whewell's model leads directly to that used by Walras, from which it is a small step to derive the offer curves devised by Marshall; for a detailed discussion and explanation of the diagrammatic links between the models, see Creedy (1990a). Marshall did not leave any statement of how he arrived at these curves, but it is of interest to compare Marshall's attempt (1975, i, pp.260-280) with the later analysis (1975, ii, pp.117-181), and finally with the mature version (1923, pp.330-360).

He began in each case with basic offer curves for each country (that are elastic over the whole length shown) and then discussed their possible shapes in terms of elasticities. In the earliest essay, Marshall used the rather clumsy expression 'guidance by the rate' for 'elasticity'. But by 1923 the analysis was clearly stated in terms of elasticities, and included a footnote giving the now standard geometrical method of finding the elasticity (1923, p.337, n.1). Consider England's offer curve in which cloth and linen are on horizontal and vertical axes respectively. If T and M are respectively the points where the tangent to the offer curve and a vertical line dropped from the point of tangency cut the horizontal axis, then the elasticity is OM/OT. The two points obviously correspond when the elasticity is unity. He also provided a method of deriving consumers' surplus from the offer curves; for discussion of this method, see Creedy (1991b). However, it seems that Marshall made no use of Whewell's treatment, as discussed below.

Marshall's recognition of the possibility of his offer curves intersecting more than once, and the circumstances under which such multiple equilibria can occur, led him to devote much energy to dynamic adjustment problems and the question of which of several equilibria would be stable. Instead of presenting the mathematics of differential equations, Marshall applied, for

the first time in economics, the now standard phase-diagram method. As
usual, and after what must have been a great deal of thought on the question, Marshall was very sceptical about the use of mathematics to examine
dynamic problems. Even if the equations of the offer curves were known precisely, he argued that 'the methods of mathematical analysis will not be able
to afford any considerable assistance in the task of determining the motion
of the exchange-index. For a large amount of additional work will have to be
done before we can obtain approximate laws for representing the magnitude
of the horizontal and vertical forces which will act upon the exchange-index in
any position' (1975, ii, p.163). Later treatments of dynamics include Samuelson (1948, pp.266-269), Bhagwati and Johnson (1960) and Amano (1968);
the latter concentrates on stability conditions.

Marshall came to regard his offer curve apparatus as capable of 'being
translated into terms of any sort of bargains between two bodies, neither of
whom is subject to any external competition in regard to those particular
bargains' (1923, p.351). A major context was that of bargaining between
firms and trade unions, but it was left to Edgeworth to extend the analysis to
those other areas. Marshall (1975, ii, p.112) contains a letter to Edgeworth of
March 1891 in which Marshall discussed the application to wage bargaining.
Edgeworth's application came as early as 1881, and was directly stimulated
by the Marshalls' *Economics of Industry* (1879) and the privately printed
chapters from the *Pure Theory*; see Creedy (1986a). Marshall also mentioned
such applications in his 1876 paper on Mill; see Pigou (1925, pp.132-133). A
distinguishing feature of Marshall's analysis of offer curves was that he also
had variations in production in mind, rather than an exchange of fixed stocks;
such variations were clarified by the detailed treatment of Meade (1952).

Marshall can also be seen at an early stage struggling with the problem
of 'triangular barter'. In some 'pages from a mathematical notebook' (1975,
ii, pp.272-274), Marshall used demand curves specified in terms of relative
prices (similar to those considered above) to examine the situation in which
Germany exchanges linen for cloth, England exchanges cloth for fur, while
Russia exchanges fur for linen. Marshall's problem was very similar to the
three-country case considered by Mill, and the approach can be seen to follow

Mill quite closely. As Mill suggested, 'everything will take place precisely as if the third country had bought German produce with her own goods, and offered that produce to England in exchange for hers' (1920, p.592). For further analysis of this case, see Creedy (1990a).

Selected material from Marshall's early work on international trade, in which he introduces offer or reciprocal demand curves, examines their properties and discusses multiple equilibria and stability issues, is given in chapter 7 below.

2.4.1 Marshall and Whewell

The question arises of whether Marshall was directly influenced by Whewell; this was first raised by Hutchison (1953, p.65). There is no reference to Whewell in any of Marshall's writings on international trade; his only reference to Whewell seems to be to the latter's role as editor of Richard Jones's works (see Pigou, 1925, p.296 and Marshall, 1975, ii, p.264). However, some writers have suggested that Marshall made use of Whewell's work; these include Henderson (1985, p.422) and Cochrane (1975, p.398). One argument to support this claim is that Marshall's signature has been found on other volumes of the *Transactions* in which Whewell's papers first appeared; see Collard (1968, p.xviii).

Further references by Marshall to Whewell have been collected by Vázquez (1995, pp.249-250). But it does not seem possible to attribute any particular analytical contributions of Marshall to the work of Whewell. Whewell (1850) showed that the King–Davenant 'law of demand' follows a third-order polynomial, yet when Marshall discussed the 'law' in the *Principles*, he simply reproduced some of Jevons's arguments; for further detail see Creedy (1986b). Whitaker, in Marshall (1975, i, p.45, n.26), noted that Marshall made no reference to Whewell's criticisms of Ricardo, but see Vázquez (1995, p.249).

While it seems surprising that Marshall was not familiar with Whewell's work, it is worth recalling a query raised by Hutchison (1950) in connection with Cournot's *Recherches*. The possible significance of Cournot's book was suggested to Jevons in 1875 by Todhunter who added that 'I never found

any person who had read the book' (Hutchison, 1950, p.8). Yet Todhunter
was, like Marshall, a Fellow of St John's College, and Marshall stated that
he read Cournot in 1868. The lack of communication between Todhunter
and Marshall on the subject of Cournot must have extended to Whewell,
about whom Todhunter also had considerable knowledge; see, for example,
Todhunter (1876). Whewell's correspondence shows that he was aware of
Cournot; on the general awareness of Cournot's work, see Vázquez (1997).

2.5   Conclusions

The aim of this chapter has been to provide an outline of the development of
the non-utility theory of exchange, beginning with the attempt by Cournot to
examine trade between two regions. This provided the starting point for the
later extension by Walras. A separate line of development starts from J.S.
Mill's international trade analysis, stimulating Whewell's mathematical version, followed some years later by Marshall's diagrammatic version. Although
no direct link can be traced from Whewell to Marshall, the indirect link is
clear in view of the influence of Whewell's analysis on Mill's later additions to
his 'great chapter'. Reference can thus be made to a Mill/Whewell/Marshall
model. Nevertheless, Walras's name can be added to this list in view of the
fact that both Marshall and Walras produced what is essentially the same
formal model of exchange, with the same properties, although they used
different diagrammatic representations of it.

Chapter 3

Utility Approaches

This chapter examines the development of a utility approach to exchange, and the associated welfare analysis of the gains from trade. It begins in section 3.1 with Jevons's exchange model and his famous 'equations of exchange'. Section 3.2 discusses Walras's utility analysis, which he provided after developing his non-utility extension of Cournot's model (discussed in chapter 2). Emphasis is placed on the nature of the different paths taken by Jevons and Walras from the same basic starting point. The synthesis and extension of Edgeworth is discussed very briefly in section 3.3. Finally, the later expositions of the theory, by Launhardt and Wicksell, are examined in section 3.4. These contributions, which turn out to be very closely related, are somewhat less well known that the other contributions.

3.1 Jevons's Equations of Exchange

Jevons, in all respects a pioneer, presented his basic exchange analysis in the context of two traders, where A and B hold endowments, a and b respectively, of goods X and Y. Where x and y are the amounts exchanged, utility after trade takes place can therefore be written as:

$$U_A = U_A(a - x, y) \tag{3.1}$$

for trader A, while for B it is:

$$U_B = U_B(x, b - y) \tag{3.2}$$

These formulations use more modern notation than that used by Jevons, who also used additive utility functions. The 'keystone' of his theory was the result that, for utility maximisation, '*the ratio of exchange of any two commodities will be the reciprocal of the ratio of the final degrees of utility of the quantities of commodity available for consumption after the exchange is complete*' (1957, p.95). This gives rise to Jevons's famous 'equations of exchange', given by:

$$-\frac{\partial U_A/\partial x}{\partial U_A/\partial y} = \frac{dy}{dx} = -\frac{\partial U_B/\partial x}{\partial U_B/\partial y} \tag{3.3}$$

The term dy/dx is the ratio of exchange of the two commodities at the margin. Jevons did not make use of constrained optimisation methods to obtain this result, but if utility is maximised subject to a 'price-taking' constraint, written as $y = px$ (from $yp_y = xp_x$), the Lagrangian is $L = U_A + \lambda(y - px)$. It is worth stressing that in this context, where x is the amount traded of the good that is given up by person A, the partial derivative $\partial U_A/\partial x$ is not marginal utility, but its negative.

Jevons recognised that integration of these differential equations presents formidable difficulties, and for this reason he restricted his attention to price-taking equilibria. He used the analogy of a lever to stress that the movement of a lever out of equilibrium also requires the difficult treatment of differential equations, but that if attention is restricted to the properties of an equilibrium, 'no such integration is applicable' (1957, p.105).

The price-taking equilibrium was examined by using his 'law of indifference', such that there are no trades at disequilibrium ratios of exchange and 'the last increments in an act of exchange must be exchanged in the same ratio as the whole quantities exchanged' (1957, p.94). This means that y/x can be substituted for dy/dx in (3.3), giving the two simultaneous equations:

$$-\frac{\partial U_A/\partial x}{\partial U_A/\partial y} = \frac{y}{x} = -\frac{\partial U_B/\partial x}{\partial U_B/\partial y} \tag{3.4}$$

Jevons recognised that y/x is equivalent to the ratio of prices of the two goods, $p = p_x/p_y = y/x$, but he preferred to leave p out of the equations until the equilibrium values of y and x have been obtained. He recognised that in general the equations in (3.4) would be nonlinear and so not capable of explicit solutions. He therefore did not take their formal analysis further, though he added the important but rather cryptic comment that the theory is 'perfectly consistent with the laws of supply and demand; and if we had the functions of utility determined, it would be possible to throw them into a form clearly expressing the equivalence of supply and demand' (1957, p.101). He went on to discuss a number of 'complex' cases, involving large and small traders, three goods and three traders, and competition between two traders, showing a confident handling of the use of the equations of exchange; for detailed discussion of these cases, see Creedy (1992a).

The discussion of price-taking behaviour (through the law of indifference) in the context of a two-person exchange model can be seen to create some 'tension' in view of the argument that there is no reason why two isolated traders should take prices as being outside their control. This point was raised by Jenkin before the publication of the *Theory of Political Economy* (see Black, 1977, iii, pp.166-178). Jevons's earlier treatment was in terms of trade between two individuals called Jones and Brown. Jenkin (1870) stimulated Jevons to publish his own work quickly. It may have been in response to this criticism that Jevons introduced the 'trading body', defined as 'any body either of buyers or sellers' (1957, p.88), as a rather awkward device to concentrate on representative traders who are price-takers. Edgeworth (1881, p.109) later described the idea more clearly as 'a sort of typical couple'.

Selections from Jevons's 1871 presentation of his exchange model and his discussion of special cases are given in chapter 6 below.

3.2 Walras, Utility and Demand

Walras's extension of the Cournot model in a non-utility framework has already been discussed in chapter 2. As Walras later stated, he 'proceeded to derive the demand curve itself from the quantities possessed by each indi-

vidual in the market and from each individual's utility curves for the two
commodities considered' (quoted by Jaffé, 1983, p.25). Hence Walras explicitly considered the step to which Jevons had alluded, but it is important to
recognise that the demands and supplies are not partial equilibrium concepts;
they refer to general equilibrium curves such as those shown in Figure 2.2.

What is surprising is that his approach, and associated demand and supply curves, seem to have been almost entirely 'lost'; they do not appear in
any history of economics or microeconomics texts. They received their most
extensive development by Launhardt (1993), whose analysis was used heavily
by Wicksell (1954), and is discussed below. The curves were discussed very
briefly in the comprehensive review of Walras's equilibrium economics by van
Daal and Jolink (1993, p.26). They commented that 'it did not get much
following', and referred to the 'undeniable complexity of the figures'. The
only treatment in general works on the history of economic analysis seems
to be the very brief mention by Stigler (1965, p. 96), who also referred to
Wicksell (but not to Launhardt).

3.2.1   Demand and Supply Curves

Walras was able to make the link from utility to demand following the crucial
advice of his colleague Paul Piccard; see Jaffé (1983, pp.303-305). What
Piccard gave Walras was essentially the 'equations of exchange' that Jevons
(1957) had earlier produced in 1871. Neither Jevons nor Walras made use of
the Lagrangian method of constrained maximisation; on the early use of this
method in economics, see Creedy (1980).

Walras's starting point is thus each of Jevons's equations in (3.4). In
particular, for trader A, the holder of good X, the relative price is:

$$p = -\frac{\partial U_A/\partial x}{\partial U_A/\partial y} \qquad (3.5)$$

Walras made the crucial step of recognising that if the substitution $y = px$ is
made where y appears anywhere on the right hand side of (3.19), it becomes
an equation containing only p and x. Hence it may be possible to solve for
x as a function of p, thereby giving A's supply curve of good X. Walras

appeared to overlook the difficulty of solving the equation in practice and he did not examine any particular utility functions.

It is precisely at this point that Walras departed from Jevons, who preferred to leave the determination of the price ratio until the final stage, after obtaining the equilibrium amounts of goods X and Y traded. This created a problem because, as mentioned above, his equations are nearly always non-linear and he fully recognised the problem of getting explicit solutions; see especially Jevons (1909, p.759). This aspect has been ignored in the literature concerned with Jevons's 'failure' to derive demand curves from utility maximisation.

This approach of Walras gives A's supply function for good X. An alternative approach would involve substituting $y = px$ into the utility functions, so that for example $U_A = U_A(a - x, px)$. Differentiating with respect to x and setting the result to zero also gives, after rearrangement, A's supply of good X as a function of p. This approach avoids the use of Lagrange multipliers. The demand for Y is obtained using the reciprocal demand relation that $y = px$. To get B's demand for good X, it is only necessary to take the result that $p = -(\partial U_B/\partial x)/(\partial U_B/\partial y)$ and again substitute for $y = px$ and solve for x as a function of p.

Although it is not always possible to solve the 'equations of exchange' for x and y, an advantage of Walras's approach is that his general equilibrium supply and demand curves can sometimes be derived explicitly. This enables the structure of the exchange model to be examined in some detail and its essential properties explored. The following subsection provides an example using the special case of constant elasticity of substitution utility functions.

Walras's introduction of a utility maximising foundation for his general equilibrium demand and supply curves, which he had previously obtained in extending Cournot's model, is given in chapter 6 below.

3.2.2 An Example: CES Utility Functions

Suppose A has the constant elasticity of substitution utility function:

$$U_A = \left\{ \alpha_1 \left(a - x\right)^{-\rho_1} + \left(1 - \alpha_1\right) y^{-\rho_1} \right\}^{-1/\rho_1} \tag{3.6}$$

where $\rho > -1$, and $\sigma_1 = 1/\left(1 + \rho_1\right)$ is the elasticity of substitution between the two goods. Differentiating with respect to x and y gives:

$$\frac{\partial U_A}{\partial x} = - \frac{\alpha_1 \left(a - x\right)^{-(1+\rho_1)} U_A}{\left\{ \alpha_1 \left(a - x\right)^{-\rho_1} + \left(1 - \alpha_1\right) y^{-\rho_1} \right\}} \tag{3.7}$$

$$\frac{\partial U_A}{\partial y} = \frac{\left(1 - \alpha_1\right) y^{-(1+\rho_1)} U_A}{\left\{ \alpha_1 \left(a - x\right)^{-\rho_1} + \left(1 - \alpha_1\right) y^{-\rho_1} \right\}} \tag{3.8}$$

Hence:

$$\frac{\partial U_A/\partial x}{\partial U_A/\partial y} = - \left(\frac{\alpha_1}{1 - \alpha_1} \right) \left(\frac{a - x}{y} \right)^{-(1+\rho_1)} \tag{3.9}$$

Person A's supply of good X, as a function of the price ratio, p, is obtained by setting $(\partial U_A/\partial x)/(\partial U_A/\partial y)$ equal to $-p$, substituting for $y = px$ and solving for x. After some manipulation it can be found that:

$$x = \frac{a}{1 + k_A p^{1 - \sigma_1}} \tag{3.10}$$

where:

$$k_A = \left(\frac{\alpha_1}{1 - \alpha_1} \right)^{\sigma_1} \tag{3.11}$$

For person B, utility is:

$$U_B = \left\{ \alpha_2 x^{-\rho_2} + \left(1 - \alpha_2\right) \left(b - y\right)^{-\rho_2} \right\}^{-1/\rho_2} \tag{3.12}$$

where $\sigma_2 = 1/\left(1 + \rho_2\right)$ is B's elasticity of substitution. Using a similar process, it can be found that B's demand for X is given by:

$$x = \frac{b/p}{1 + \left(\frac{1}{k_B} \right) p^{\sigma_2 - 1}} \tag{3.13}$$

where:

$$k_B = \left(\frac{\alpha_2}{1 - \alpha_2} \right)^{\sigma_2} \tag{3.14}$$

It is not possible to solve analytically for the equilibrium price for which A's supply is equal to B's demand for good X. Inspection of the shape of the supply and demand functions shows, however, that there is only one equilibrium solution. The demand curve for X is always downward sloping and the supply curve is always upward sloping if the elasticity of substitution, σ_1, is greater than unity. If the elasticity is less than unity, then the supply curve is backward bending over the whole of the range, while the demand curve continues to slope downwards.

A richer range of possibilities exists if individuals hold some of both goods before trade takes place. For example, if person A holds a_1 and b_1 respectively of goods X and Y before trade, then in the supply curve of good X the numerator is changed from a to $a_1 - b_1 k_A p^{-\sigma_1}$. If person B holds a_2 and b_2 of X and Y respectively, then it can be found that the demand curve has a numerator of $(b_2/p) - (a_2/k_B) p^{\sigma_2 - 1}$ instead of simply b/p. While the demand curve is still downward sloping for all values of σ_2, the supply curve has both upward sloping and backward bending sections, so long as $\sigma_1 < 1$. In this case it is possible for multiple equilibria to occur. Further examples of this approach using a range of utility functions are given in Creedy (1996, pp.40-49).

3.2.3 Walras Lost and Found

The subsequent neglect of Walras's approach is unfortunate in view of its usefulness. For example, it shows how 'backward bending' supply curves can arise in a 'natural way'; it was in the context of the backward bending supply curve of labour that Buchanan (1971) referred to the modern treatment in terms of 'doctrinal retrogression'. It is possible, though unlikely, that Robbins's (1930) treatment of the supply curve of labour was influenced by Walras, indirectly through Wicksell, with whose work he was much more familiar. The direct influence of Wicksteed (1933) on Robbins is most likely, but even here there may be an indirect influence of Walras. The backward bending curves show immediately how multiple equilibria can arise. The recognition of such multiple equilibria led Walras to his famous analysis of stability.

The usefulness of the approach is perhaps also demonstrated by the fact that similar curves have been independently reinvented several times. For example, Viner (1955, pp. 538-541) used similar curves to explain an international trade argument of J.S. Mill (and in a long footnote derived the relationships between the relevant elasticities), although Viner did not show any backward bending curves. Vickrey (1964, pp.105-108) derived such curves directly from the Edgeworth box diagram. Atkinson and Stiglitz (1980, p.189) derived the general equilibrium curves directly from special utility functions suggested by Shapley and Shubik (1977); but they made no reference to Walras.

These 'rediscoveries' are of course in the context of exchange and general equilibrium. While modern general equilibrium theory has established the full conditions required for the existence and uniqueness of equilibrium, the development of the theory did not actually proceed in a direct line from Walras. Indeed, the early stimulus came from Cassel, who quickly arranged for his work to be translated into English and did not acknowledge that his simplified general equilibrium model was taken from Walras; see, for example, Weintraub (1985). Phelps Brown (1936) based his valuable introductory exposition of general equilibrium analysis on Cassel without being aware that it was from Walras.

3.3   Edgeworth: The Apogee

Edgeworth, directly stimulated by his personal contact with Jevons, provided a majestic synthesis and extension of the exchange model in his highly original *Mathematical Psychics* (1881). Jevons (1957, p.96) commented that 'it is hardly possible to represent this theory completely by means of a diagram', but of course Edgeworth provided such an apparatus with his indifference curves and contract curve contained within his 'box diagram'. This is sometimes known as an Edgeworth-Bowley box, following the later exposition by Bowley (1924), who achieved the distinction of being even more terse than Edgeworth. He also linked the offer curves directly to indifference curves.

The technical device of the box diagram, after a very slow start, has now become ubiquitous in microeconomic theory.

A price-taking, or competitive, equilibrium is shown in Figure 3.1, which shows pre-trade indifference curves, offer curves, and the mutual tangency of indifference curves with the price line. Edgeworth emphasised the role of the number of traders, stressed that indeterminacy arises with small numbers so that there is a need for arbitration, and showed that the utilitarian objective, as a principle of arbitration, specifies a position on the contract curve and is acceptable to risk averse traders, thereby foreshadowing the later 'neo-contractarian' utilitarian approach. For a comparison of alternative types of exchange equilibria, including price-taking, utilitarian and bargaining solutions, see Creedy (1994b).

Edgeworth also showed how increasing the number of traders using barter, with individuals following a recontracting process in which provisional bargains can be broken and coalitions can be formed, causes the range of indeterminacy along the contract curve to shrink until, with many traders, only the price-taking equilibria remain. All this was achieved at great speed and expressed in a highly individual style; for further discussion, see Creedy (1986a). Selections from Edgeworth (1881) are given in chapter 7.

3.4 Later Expositions

Two of the most comprehensive expositions of the theory of exchange were made towards the end of the century, by Launhardt (1993) in 1885 and Wicksell (1954) in 1893. Neither writer seems to have read Edgeworth (1881), although Wicksell was familiar with the contract curve from Marshall's *Principles*. Unfortunately it was many years before their works were translated into English. The first of these was Wicksell who, despite his strong criticisms of Launhardt, made extensive use of his book and cannot properly be understood without reference to Launhardt's analysis. Walrasian supply and demand curves were first derived formally in 1885 from utility functions by Launhardt (1993), who used the assumption of quadratic utility functions and demonstrated the properties diagrammatically much more clearly than

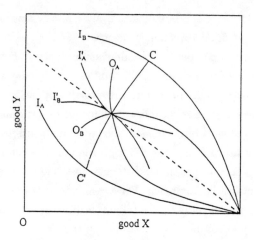

Figure 3.1: A Price-taking Equilibrium

Walras. He also used the results to examine disequilibrium trading and its welfare effects. Indeed Launhardt's study can claim to be the first systematic treatise on modern welfare economics. Selections from his book are given in chapter 8 below.

3.4.1 Launhardt's Exchange Analysis

Launhardt's analysis, starting from the exchange models of Jevons and Walras, is noteworthy for his derivation from explicit utility functions of algebraic forms of general equilibrium supply and demand curves expressed as functions of relative prices. Whereas Jevons and Walras concentrated on the price-taking equilibrium properties of their exchange models, Launhardt explored a process of disequilibrium trading in which successive trades take place at the 'short end' of the market, that is, the minimum of supply and demand at a price. His main concern was, however, to examine the welfare aspects of exchange, comparing the gains from trade under competitive and monopolistic behaviour. Launhardt has been criticised for suggesting that aggregate utility, and thus the aggregate gain from trade, is maximised at the price-taking equilibrium; see, for example, Wicksell (1954, p.76, n.2; 1934, p.81, n.1). For further discussion of the utilitarian optimum, along with price-taking and bargaining solutions, see Creedy (1994b). Launhardt nevertheless showed that a process of disequilibrium trading, in which the price initially favours the relatively poorer individual, can improve the aggregate gains from trade compared with the price-taking equilibrium.

3.4.2 Utility, Demand and Supply Functions

Instead of restricting attention to general results, Launhardt wished to illustrate the nature of the exchange model in more detail using explicit utility functions. Following Jevons, he assumed additive utility functions. As an engineer, it would have been natural to start with utility as a polynomial function of amounts consumed. The argument that marginal utility decreases steadily as consumption increases, with reference to Jevons's example of water, leads automatically to the quadratic form. Write A's utility as:

$$U_A (a - x, y) = \alpha_A (a - x) - \beta_A (a - x)^2 + \gamma_A y - \delta_A y^2 \tag{3.15}$$

Substituting $y = px$ in (3.15) gives A's utility in terms of x and p:[1]

$$U_A = \alpha_A (a - x) - \beta_A (a - x)^2 + \gamma_A px - \delta_A (px)^2 \tag{3.16}$$

The marginal rate of substitution is a ratio of linear functions of x and y, so it is known, following the later work of Allen and Bowley (1935), that the expenditure on each good is a linear function of total expenditure, with coefficients depending on prices.

A's supply function can be derived by maximising U_A with respect to x, for given relative price, p. Setting $dU_A/dx = 0$ gives, after rearrangement:

$$x = \frac{\gamma_A p - (\alpha_A - 2a\beta_A)}{2 (\beta_A + \delta_A p^2)} \tag{3.17}$$

A's demand for good Y is obtained by substituting into $y = px$. If B has the utility function:

$$U_B (x, b - y) = \alpha_B x - \beta_B x^2 + \gamma_B (b - y) - \delta_B (b - y)^2 \tag{3.18}$$

---

[1]See Launhardt (1993, p.36).

then B's demand for X may be obtained by substituting $y = px$ into (3.18) and maximising U_B with respect to x, giving:

$$x = \frac{\alpha_B - p(\gamma_B - 2\delta_B b)}{2(\beta_B + \delta_B p^2)} \qquad (3.19)$$

Equations (3.17) and (3.19) are the equivalent of Launhardt's results in (1993, pp.36-38).

Equating (3.17) and (3.19) shows that the equilibrium relative price is the root or roots of a cubic equation, but Launhardt (1993, p.43) made the simplifying assumption that the two individuals have identical tastes, differing only in their pre-trade endowments of the goods. Setting $\alpha_A = \alpha_B = \alpha$, and so on, the denominators of both (3.17) and (3.19) become identical, so that the term in p^2 cancels and the equilibrium price is:

$$p = \frac{\alpha - \beta a}{\gamma - \delta b} \qquad (3.20)$$

Hence the price depends only on the parameters of the utility functions and the total stocks of the goods available. This result has important implications for the following subsection.

Further insight into the price-taking equilibrium in this special case, not discussed by Launhardt, can be obtained by noting that A's marginal utility of good X is equal to $\alpha - 2\beta(a - x)$, while B's marginal utility is $\alpha - 2\beta x$. The arithmetic mean marginal utility is thus $\alpha - \beta a$, the numerator of (3.20). Similarly, the arithmetic mean utility of good Y is the denominator of (3.20). Hence the equilibrium price is the ratio of the arithmetic mean marginal utility of good X to that of good Y.

3.4.3   Disequilibrium Trading

Whereas previous writers restricted attention to price-taking behaviour, Launhardt examined the implications of disequilibrium trading. This was in terms of 'repeated exchange' in which, starting from a disequilibrium price, there is gradual adjustment towards an equilibrium. With excess demand or supply, trade is assumed to take place at the 'short end' of the market, the minimum of supply and demand. At each stage of the price-adjustment process, there

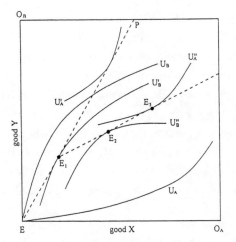

Figure 3.2: Disequilibrium Trading

is a change in the allocation of goods between the two individuals. But in the case of identical individuals, such changes can have no effect on the final equilibrium price because, as shown by (3.20), this depends only on the parameters of the common utility functions and the total stocks. This result does not hold if the individuals have different tastes: see Creedy (1994a).

Another example of a situation in which trading at disequilibrium, or false, prices does not affect the equilibrium price was later produced by Marshall, although the precise structure of Marshall's example only became evident in the debate with Edgeworth; see Creedy (1990b). If utility functions are additive and the marginal utility of one of the goods is constant, it can be shown that the final total amount of the other good traded and the final relative price are independent of the sequence of disequilibrium trades. However, the amount traded of the good for which marginal utility is constant does depend on the sequence of trades. This result holds irrespective of the form of the individuals' utility functions for the good which does not have constant marginal utility.

The type of disequilibrium trading described by Launhardt, and later by Marshall, can be illustrated by an extension of a diagram suggested by Edge-

worth; see Marshall (1961, p.844). This type of process was also discussed
by Johnson (1913), who made no references to earlier literature. An example
is shown in Figure 3.2, where the endowment position moves from E to E_1,
and then E_2. With the price line EP, there is an excess supply of good X
and trade takes place at the demand corresponding to point E_1. At the lower
price, represented by the line $E_1 P_1$ drawn through the new endowment point,
the excess supply of X is lower than formerly and the new trade takes place
at the point E_2, the minimum of supply and demand. Each disequilibrium
trade is a Pareto improvement and the sequence of trades, bounded by the
pre-trade indifference curves, must converge to an equilibrium somewhere on
the contract curve.

3.4.4   Individual Gains from Trade

Launhardt emphasised disequilibrium trading in order to examine its effect
on the gains from trade. The assumption of common preferences made it
much easier for him to provide numerical illustrations. His main focus was
on the difference between alternative allocative mechanisms. He began by
comparing the price ratio that maximises an individual's gains from trade
with the equilibrium price ratio. Consider A, who begins by holding all the
stocks of good X, and achieves a gain in utility resulting from trade, G_A, of:

$$G_A \;=\; U_A\left(a - x, y\right) - U_A\left(a, 0\right)$$
$$=\; \gamma_A y - \delta_A y^2 - \left(\alpha_A - 2\beta_A a\right) x - \beta_A x^2 \qquad (3.21)$$

Substituting $y = px$ into (3.21) gives Launhardt's (1993, p.46) result that:

$$G_A = x\left\{\gamma_A p - \left(\alpha_A - 2\beta_A a\right)\right\} - x^2\left(\beta_A + \delta_A p^2\right) \qquad (3.22)$$

After producing the equivalent of (3.22), Launhardt substituted numerical
values for the coefficients in utility functions and used the assumption of
identical tastes in order to obtain G_A in terms of p and p^2. The value of
p which maximises G_A turns out to be the positive root of a quadratic.
However, he did not explain the precise method, giving only the numerical
solution. Launhardt showed with his numerical examples that the price ratio

which maximises A's gain from trade (with a single transaction taking place at that price) is different from the price-taking equilibrium value. However, the total gain of both A and B at that point is less than at the price-taking equilibrium. Launhardt had therefore examined the equivalent of A's 'optimum tariff' or monopoly price.

Further insight can be obtained by differentiating (3.22) with respect to p, which gives, after collecting terms:

$$\frac{dG_A}{dp} = x\gamma_A - 2x^2\delta_A p + \frac{dx}{dp}\left\{\gamma_A p - (\alpha_A - 2\beta_A a) - 2x\left(\beta_A + \delta_A p^2\right)\right\} \quad (3.23)$$

By taking the term $2\left(\beta_A - \delta_A p^2\right)$ outside the curly brackets in (3.23) it can be seen that:

$$\frac{dG_A}{dp} = \gamma_A x - 2x^2\delta_A p + 2\left(\beta_A + \delta_A p^2\right)\left\{\frac{\gamma_A p - (\alpha_A - 2\beta_A a)}{2\left(\beta_A + \delta_A p^2\right)} - x\right\}\frac{dx}{dp} \quad (3.24)$$

The first term in the curly brackets in (3.24) is equal to A's supply of good X at price p. However, it is important to recognise that the xs in (3.24) must refer to the demand for good X by person B. This is because, for disequilibrium prices, trading must take place at the 'short end' of the market, and for prices that are favourable to person A, there is an excess supply of good X. By setting dG_A/dp equal to zero, and substituting for x from B's demand function in (3.19), the price that maximises A's gain from trade is the root of a rather complex expression. It is, however, clear that the equilibrium price, for which the term in curly brackets in (3.24) is zero, does not correspond to the price for which G_A is a maximum, for which the whole of the right hand side of (3.24) must be zero.

If individuals are identical (except for their endowments of goods), the gains from trade are equal if all trade takes place at the price-taking equilibrium price. This can be seen by writing B's gains as:

$$\begin{aligned} G_B &= U(x, b-y) - U(0, b) \\ &= x\left\{\alpha_B - (\gamma_B - 2\delta_B b)p\right\} - x^2\left(\beta_B + \delta_B p^2\right) \end{aligned} \quad (3.25)$$

Substituting for the price-taking equilibrium price from (3.20), it can be seen from (3.22) and (3.25), and remembering that the supply and demand for X

must now be equal, that $G_A = G_B$. Launhardt (1993, pp.45-46) did not give such a proof, but showed that the gains are equal using his numerical example and pointed out that the result holds only for the special assumptions.

3.4.5   Price-taking and Aggregate Utility

Launhardt's examination of exchange contained the unfortunate and incorrect argument that 'It is simple to prove that in an exchange at equilibrium the sum of the utility for both proprietors, that is the utility achieved in an overall economic sense, has reached a maximum' (1993, p.43). Launhardt's discussion was terse, with a lack of clarity that is uncharacteristic of his work; for further analysis of Launhardt's spurious argument, see Creedy (1994a). But he immediately qualified this statement, and the qualification was based on his analysis of a sequence of trades rather than a single exchange transaction. Launhardt's slip provided an easy target for later critics such as Wicksell.

Launhardt would have avoided the problem if he had attempted to solve for the values of x and y which maximise U. Total utility, as above, is given by:

$$U = U_A + U_B = U_A\left(a - x, y\right) + U_B\left(x, b - y\right) \qquad (3.26)$$

In view of the assumption of additivity, the partial derivatives $\partial\left(U_A + U_B\right)/\partial x$ and $\partial\left(U_A + U_B\right)/\partial y$ depend only on x and y respectively. Hence the two first-order conditions for the maximisation of U can be solved explicitly for x and y, as:

$$x = \frac{\left(\alpha_B - \alpha_A\right) + 2\beta_A a}{2\left(\beta_A + \beta_B\right)} \qquad (3.27)$$

$$y = \frac{\left(\gamma_A - \gamma_B\right) + 2\delta_B b}{2\left(\delta_B + \delta_A\right)} \qquad (3.28)$$

These values of x and y do not equal the competitive equilibrium values. The competitive equilibrium involves voluntary trading on the part of individuals attempting to maximise their utility, subject to given prices, whereas alternative solutions involve the amounts traded being imposed on individuals. When criticising Launhardt, Wicksell (1934, p.81, n.1) pointed out that, with

Table 3.1: The Pre-trade Situation

	Person		
	A	B	Total
Stock of good X	400	0	400
Stock of good Y	0	480	480
Utility	240	576	816

identical tastes, total utility is maximised when the parties 'simply exchange half their stocks'. This is confirmed by appropriate substitution into (3.27) and (3.28) giving a rate of exchange, y/x, of b/a, which obviously differs from that resulting from equation (3.20) above.

Launhardt assumed that the values of α, β, γ and δ, the parameters of common utility functions, are 1.0, 0.001, 1.8 and 0.00125 respectively. He stated these in terms of fractions, which would have been more convenient when making calculations with pencil and paper. The pre-trade situation is shown in Table 3.1 where, for example, A's pre-trade endowment of 400 units of good X gives utility of 240. The values in the tables have been obtained using a computer, and show that Launhardt's own calculations are accurate, though they would have been tedious to produce. The price-taking equilibrium and the values which maximise aggregate utility, the utilitarian solution, are shown in the first two rows of Table 3.2. For identical tastes the utilitarian position involves equal sharing of the goods, and person B is worse off than before any trade takes place. Despite the fact that aggregate utility is maximised, there is no constraint requiring non-negative gains. The equilibrium price for price-taking may be obtained from equation (3.20) as 0.5. The assumption of identical preferences means that both individuals obtain a gain from trade of 93.33. Aggregate utility is less than with the utilitarian arrangement, as shown in the final column of Table 3.2. The utilitarian arrangement was not examined directly by Launhardt since he had incorrectly concluded that it coincides with the price-taking equilibrium.

Launhardt contrasted the equilibrium with a sequence of trades and monopoly pricing. For the latter, substitution into A's gain from trade, given by equation (3.22), using B's demand for X from equation (3.19) to

Table 3.2: Launhardt's Sequence of Trades

	p	x	y	U_A	U_B	$U_A + U_B$
Utilitarian	-	200	240	520	520	1040
Price-taking	0.50	266.67	133.33	333.33	669.33	1002.66
Trade 1.	0.78	151.09	117.85	381.73	616.19	997.92
Trade 2.	0.50	95.43	47.71	393.68	628.14	1021.82
Trade 1.	0.43	233.12	100.24	306.91	682.07	988.98
Trade 2.	0.50	41.32	20.66	309.15	684.31	993.46

substitute for x, gives rise to A's gain in terms of the price ratio as:

$$G_A = \frac{-2520p^2 + 5040p - 1400}{4 + 5p^2} \tag{3.29}$$

Launhardt (1993, p.46) gave this equation and stated without discussion that G_A reaches a maximum for $p = 0.78$. Differentiation of G_A with respect to p and rearrangement shows that this price can be obtained as the positive root of a quadratic. The situation after trading at this price is shown in the third row of Table 3.2, where person A has utility of 381.73, which exceeds that obtained from the price-taking equilibrium. Trader A gains 141.73 while B gains 40.19 from the trade at $p = 0.78$. However, aggregate utility is less than at the price-taking equilibrium.

This single trade does not exhaust all the potential gains from trade, and further trades can take place at prices lower than 0.78. Launhardt assumed that the next trade took place at the equilibrium price, and with identical tastes this is independent of the earlier trade. Hence the second trade occurs at $p = 0.5$ and the result is given in the fourth line of Table 3.2. The aggregate gain as a result of the two trades is 1021.82 and is higher than in the price-taking equilibrium. It is indeed this result which gives Launhardt's qualification to his earlier argument.

A similar approach shows that the monopoly price set by person B is $p = 0.43$. The resulting sequence of trades is shown in the last two rows of Table 3.2. The sequence of trades can be seen using an Edgeworth box. The monopoly price involves a tangency position between an indifference curve of the monopolist and the other trader's offer curve, but this is not on the

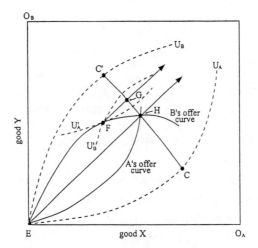

Figure 3.3: Launhardt's Sequence of Two Trades

contract curve so the second trade involves a movement to the contract curve. Launhardt also examined the limits of the contract curve; the intersection of the linear contract curve with quadratic pre-trade indifference curves. The sequence of the two trades is shown in Figure 3.3.

3.4.6 Wicksell's Examples

Wicksell (1954) relied heavily on Launhardt's treatment. However, he saw clearly that aggregate utility is not maximised at the price-taking equilibrium, and for this reason was strongly critical of Launhardt; see Wicksell (1954, p.18). However, Wicksell's discussion of disequilibrium trading can only be understood with reference to Launhardt's treatment. Wicksell produced his own numerical examples of a sequence of trades, assumed values for α, β, γ and δ of 200, 5, 10 and 0.5 respectively, and supposed that trader A holds 10 units of X while B holds 100 units of Y. He stated that the equation of the contract curve is $10x + 3y = 200$.

Substituting into the equivalent of (3.20), Wicksell obtained the equilibrium price ratio of 30. Substitution for $p = 30$ into equation (3.17), and using $y = 30x$, gives equilibrium amounts traded as $x = 2$ and $y = 60$, where

Table 3.3: Wicksell's Example

	p	x	y	U_A	U_B	$U_A + U_B$
Utilitarian	-	5	50	1250	1250	2500
Price-taking	30	2	60	1700	700	2400
Trade 1.	13	1.115	14.498	1516.73	706.32	2223.05
Trade 2.	$17\frac{2}{3}$	0.968	17.105	1536.05	845.05	2381.10
Trade 3.	22	0.508	11.165	1543.57	893.17	2436.74
Trade 4.	30	0.458	13.736	1554.05	903.65	2457.70

both traders gain 200 units of utility.[2] Wicksell did not present the equations of the demand and supply curves, however. Instead of goods X and Y, he used oxen and sheep respectively and stated, 'supposing that he [A] was first expected to exchange 1 ox for 13 sheep, then a second ox for $17\frac{2}{3}$ sheep, then $\frac{1}{2}$ ox for 11 sheep and finally another $\frac{1}{2}$ ox for 15 sheep, then there would remain for him after each exchange respectively a proportion of exchange between sheep and oxen [marginal rate of substitution] of more than 1 : 13, 1 : $17\frac{2}{3}$, 1 : 22 and finally of just 1 : 30, so that each single exchange would have to seem to him undoubtedly profitable, although he has in fact finally exchanged just 3 oxen for not quite 57 sheep' (1954, p. 67).

The final result is that B gets more oxen (good X) and gives up fewer sheep (good Y) in comparison with the price-taking equilibrium. Wicksell's terse discussion of this sequence of disequilibrium trades is misleading and conceals much numerical work. For example, he supposes that A is first expected to exchange 1 ox for 13 sheep. But if the price ratio is 13, it is shown in Table 3.3 that 1.115 units of X are traded for 14.498 units of Y. The ratio, y/x, is equal to the price ratio, but the trade that person A prefers is not quite the same as in Wicksell's example. Similarly, when the price is $17\frac{2}{3}$, A does not actually wish to trade 1 ox for $17\frac{2}{3}$ sheep, but 0.968 ox for 17.105 sheep. There is also a discrepancy in the other trades, given the prices mentioned by Wicksell, and in total 3.049 oxen are traded for 56.504 sheep. Following the sequence of disequilibrium trades, A is slightly better off than in the pre-trade position, having gained 54.05 units of utility from

---

[2]There is a misprint in Wicksell (1954, p.66) which gives $x = 30y$.

the trades overall, but B's gain from trade is, at 403.65, over double that obtained from the price-taking equilibrium. The conclusion is similar to that of Launhardt. When the disequilibrium trades favour the poorer person, in this case trader B, total utility is greater than in the competitive solution. The fact that Wicksell did not make it clear that he had followed Launhardt and uncharacteristically poured scorn on his work simultaneously made his own contribution less transparent and damaged the reputation of Launhardt. Selections from Wicksell's 1893 treatment are given in chapter 8 below.

3.5 Conclusions

The aim of this chapter has been to provide an outline of the development of utility approaches to the theory of exchange, which culminated in the contribution of Edgeworth. The importance of exchange, viewed as the central economic problem for the early neoclassical economists, was stressed in chapter 1. Jevons's and Walras's utility approaches were examined, showing the different paths they took from the same basic equations of exchange. After a very brief discussion of Edgeworth, the neglected but valuable contribution of Launhardt, along with the later work of Wicksell, was examined. Emphasis was placed on the similarity of the formal structure of the exchange model used by the various writers. This similarity has been obscured by the different forms of presentation used and the emphasis given to various aspects and results by each investigator.

Part III

Selections from the Texts

Chapter 4

The Demand Function

4.1 Cournot

This section contains material from chapter IV of Cournot (1927, pp.47-55), first published in 1838, where he defines demand curves and examines their properties, in particular the variation in total revenue with price. Revenue is maximised at the point of unit elasticity, but Cournot did not produce the concept of price elasticity.

Of The Law of Demand

Let us admit therefore that the sales or the annual demand D is, for each article, a particular function $F(p)$ of the price p of such article. To know the form of this function would be to know what we call the *law of demand* or *of sales*. It depends evidently on the kind of utility of the article, on the nature of the services it can render or the enjoyments it can procure, on the habits and customs of the people, on the average wealth, and on the scale on which wealth is distributed.

Since so many moral causes capable of neither enumeration nor measurement affect the law of demand, it is plain that we should no more expect this law to be expressible by an algebraic formula than the law of mortality, and all the laws whose determination enters into the field of statistics, or what is called social arithmetic. Observation must therefore be depended on for furnishing the means of drawing up between proper limits a table of the corresponding values of D and p; after which, by the well-known methods of interpolation or by graphic processes, an empiric formula or a curve can be made to represent the function in question; and the solution of problems can be pushed as far as numerical applications.

But even if this object were unattainable (on account of the difficulty of obtaining observations of sufficient number and accuracy, and also on account of the progressive variations which the law of demand must undergo in a country which has not yet reached a practically stationary condition), it would be nevertheless not improper to introduce the unknown law of demand into analytical combinations, by means of an indeterminate symbol; for it is well known that one of the most important functions of analysis consists precisely in assigning determinate relations between quantities to which numerical values and even algebraic forms are absolutely unassignable.

Unknown functions may none the less possess properties or general characteristics which are known; as, for instance, to be indefinitely increasing or decreasing, or periodical, or only real between certain limits. Nevertheless such data, however imperfect they may seem, by reason of their very generality and by means of analytical symbols, may lead up to relations equally general which would have been difficult to discover without this help. Thus without knowing the law of decrease of the capillary forces, and starting solely from the principle that these forces are inappreciable at appreciable distances, mathematicians have demonstrated the general laws of the phenomena of capillarity, and these laws have been confirmed by observation.

On the other hand, by showing what determinate relations exist between unknown quantities, analysis reduces these unknown quantities to the smallest possible number, and guides the observer to the best observations for discovering their values. It reduces and coordinates statistical documents; and it diminishes the labour of statisticians at the same time that it throws light on them.

For instance, it is impossible *a priori* to assign an algebraic form to the law of mortality; it is equally impossible to formulate the function expressing the subdivision of population by ages in a stationary population; but these two functions are connected by so simple a relation, that, as soon as statistics have permitted the construction of a table of mortality, it will be possible, without recourse to new observations, to deduce from this table one expressing the proportion of the various ages in the midst of a stationary population, or even of a population for which the annual excess of deaths over births is known.

Who doubts that in the field of social economy there is a mass of figures thus mutually connected by assignable relations, by means of which the easiest to determine empirically might be chosen, so as to deduce all the others from it by means of theory?

We will assume that the function $F(p)$, which expresses the law of demand or of the market, is a *continuous* function, *i.e.* a function which does not pass suddenly from one value to another, but which takes in passing all intermediate values ...

If the function $F(p)$ is continuous, it will have the property common to all functions of this nature, and on which so many important applications of mathematical analysis are based: *the variations of the demand will be sensibly proportional to the variations in price so long as these last are small fractions of the original price.* Moreover, these variations will be of opposite signs, *i.e.* an increase in price will correspond with a diminution of the demand ...

Since the function $F(p)$ is continuous, the function $pF(p)$, which expresses the total value of the quantity annually sold, must be continuous also. This function would equal zero if p equals zero, since the consumption of any article remains finite even on the hypothesis that it is absolutely free; or, in other words, it is theoretically always possible to assign to the symbol p a value so small that the product $pF(p)$ will vary imperceptibly from zero. The function $pF(p)$ disappears also when p becomes infinite, or, in other words, theoretically a value can always be assigned to p so great that the demand for the article and the production of it would cease. Since the function $pF(p)$ at first increases, and then decreases as p increases, there is therefore a value of p which makes this function a maximum, and which is given by the equation,

$$F(p) + pF'(p) = 0 \qquad (4.1)$$

in which F, according to Lagrange's notation, denotes the differential coefficient of function F.

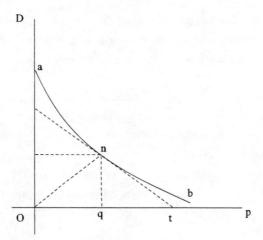

Figure 4.1: Demand and Maximum Revenue

If we lay out the curve *anb* in Figure 4.1, of which the abscissas *oq* and the ordinates *qn* represent the variables p and D, the root of equation (4.1) will be the abscissa of the point n from which the triangle *ont*, formed by the tangent *nt* and the radius vector *on*, is isosceles, so that we have $oq = qt$.

We may admit that it is impossible to determine the function $F(p)$ empirically for each article, but it is by no means the case that the same obstacles prevent the approximate determination of the value of p which satisfies equation (4.1) or which renders the product $pF(p)$ a maximum. The construction of a table, where these values could be found, would be the work best calculated for preparing for the practical and rigorous solution of questions relating to the theory of wealth.

But even if it were impossible to obtain from statistics the value of p which should render the product $pF(p)$ a maximum, it would be easy to learn, at least for all articles to which the attempt has been made to extend commercial statistics, whether current prices are above or below this value. Suppose that when the price becomes $p + \Delta p$, the annual consumption as shown by statistics, such as customhouse records, becomes $D - \Delta D$. According as

$$\frac{\Delta D}{\Delta p} < \text{ or } > \frac{D}{p}$$

the increase in price, Δp, will increase or diminish the product $pF(p)$; and, consequently, it will be known whether the two values p and $p+\Delta p$ (assuming Δp to be a small function of p) fall above or below the value which makes the product under consideration a maximum.

Commercial statistics should therefore be required to separate articles of high economic importance into two categories, according as their current prices are above or below the value which makes a maximum of $pF(p)$. We shall see that many economic problems have different solutions, according as the article in question belongs to one or the other of these two categories.

We know by the theory of maxima and minima that equation (4.1) is satisfied as well by the values of p which render $pF(p)$ a minimum as by those which render this product a maximum. The argument used at the beginning of the preceding article shows, indeed, that the function $pF(p)$ necessarily has a maximum, but it might have several and pass through minimum values between. A root of equation (4.1) corresponds to a maximum or a minimum according as

$$2F'(p) + pF''(p) < \text{ or } > 0,$$

or, substituting for p its value and considering the essentially negative sign of $F'(p)$,

$$2[F(p)]^2 - F(p) \times f''(p) > \text{ or } < 0$$

In consequence, whenever $F''(p)$ is negative, or when the curve $D = F(p)$ turns its concave side to the axis of the abscissas, it is impossible that there should be a minimum, nor more than one maximum. In the contrary case, the existence of several maxima or minima is not proved to be impossible.

But if we cease considering the question from an exclusively abstract standpoint, it will be instantly recognized how improbable it is that the function $pF(p)$ should pass through several intermediate maxima and minima inside of the limits between which the value of p can vary; and as it is unnecessary to consider maxima which fall beyond these limits, if any such exist, all problems are the same as if the function $pF(p)$ only admitted a single maximum. The essential question is always whether, for the extent of the limits of oscillation of p, the function $pF(p)$ is increasing or decreasing for increasing values of p.

4.2   Whewell

This section contains material from Whewell (1850, pp.1-7) where he specifies the change in expenditure resulting from a price change, in terms of the 'specific rate of change' of the commodity. The specification is used in his trade model; see chapter 5 below.

Mathematical Exposition of some Doctrines of Political Economy

The questions which I now intend to consider are some which relate to the connection of demand, supply, and price, whether in the same country, or in different countries. And, first, in the same country. That the price of any commodity depends upon the relation of the demand and the supply is commonly and truly stated. Put in order to express this dependence in a mathematical manner, we must define with precision the quantities which enter into the relation.

Let p be the price of commodity C, and q the quantity effectually demanded, that is, bought, at the price; p being of course expressed in units of money, and q in terms of some unit which measures the commodity C.

The demand for C depends (ceteris paribus) upon the price: q depends upon p. Let p increase in any ratio: the demand that is the quantity which buyers are willing to purchase, will commonly diminish: but it may diminish either in the same ratio in which the price increases or less rapidly ...

In order to express such a relation generally, let p become $p' = p(1 + x)$, and let q become q', such that $p'q' = pq(1 + mx)$, where m is a certain coefficient ...

But the price may also be considered as depending on the supply, that is, on the quantity supplied for sale: and the quantity supplied to buyers at a given price is the same as the quantity bought at that price; therefore the equation just given, $p'q' = pq\,(1 + mx)$, expresses the relation between supply (q') and price (p').

Which of these classes of cases is likely to exist in practice?

It will be apparent, on consideration, that one or other will occur according to the nature of commodity, and thus, that m has different values for different commodities. We shall endeavour to indicate certain classes of commodities according to this relation.

(A) There may be some commodities on which, in a given society the same sum is expended whatever be the price of the article (per unit); a smaller quantity being bought exactly in proportion as the price is higher. Such would be the case with ornamental attire, for instance, if each person or if persons on an average were to spend upon it a determinate sum every year; an *allowance for dress,* as it might be termed. In this case, when p becomes $p(1 + x), p'q'$, the money demand, remains unaltered, whence $pq\,(1 + mx) = pq$. Here $m = 0$.

(B) There may be other commodities of which the quantity bought is the same whatever be the price: such, for example, may be articles which are looked upon as necessary by rich persons; as, for instance, official dresses and conventional appendages of persons in office, and the like. Here when p becomes $p\,(1 + x)$, q remains unaltered. Therefore $pq\,(1 + mx) = pq\,(1 + x)$. Here $m = 1$.

(C) There are other commodities of which the price increases more rapidly than the quantity supplied diminishes: for instance, the general necessaries of life ...

The more we suppose prices to rise for a given diminution of supply, the more will m approach to 1 ...

In all these cases m is between 0 and 1.

(D) There may be other commodities of which the price increases in a less proportion than the supply diminishes: or as the case is perhaps more evident, there may be commodities of which when the price diminishes, the demand increases, and in so great a proportion that the whole sum expended on them is greater than before. This may be the case with some luxuries ...

In all these cases m is negative.

If it were possible to arrange commodities according to the value of m, the specific rate of change, (as is done hypothetically for the sake of example in the above instances) so that we should for every quantity know the value of m, we might solve a great variety of problems respecting the variations of price, of demand, and of supply, so far as these quantities depend on each other. And so far as the formulae are applicable, we have the equations

$$p' = p\left(1 + x\right), p'q' = pq\left(1 + mx\right), q' = q\frac{1 + mx}{1 + x}$$

It is well observed by Mr. J. S. Mill (*Polit. Econ. i. 529*) that instead of saying, as writers have often said, that the price depends upon the *ratio* of demand and supply, we ought rather to say that the price depends upon the *equation* of demand and supply. And we may apply the term, *the equation of demand and supply* to the equation

$$p'q' = pq\left(1 + mx\right)$$

Chapter 5

International Trade Models

5.1 Cournot

This section contains material from chapter X of Cournot (1927, pp.117-121), first published in 1838, where he examines trade between two regions involving a single good.

Of The Communication of Markets

The perfecting of commerce and of means of transportation, and the abolition of prohibitory laws or restrictive taxes, may put into communication markets which were previously isolated from each other, either wholly or only with reference to certain commodities. The object of this chapter is to study the principal consequences which the establishment of such communication may involve.

It is evident that an article capable of transportation must flow from the market where its value is less to the market where its value is greater, until this difference in value, from one market to the other, represents no more than the cost of transportation.

By cost of transportation must be understood, not only the price of necessaries and the wages of the agents by whom the transportation is mechanically carried on, but also insurance premiums, and the profits of the merchant, who ought to obtain in his business the interest on the capital employed and a proper return for his industry.

To compare the values of the commodity in the two markets, it is necessary to consider not only the prices of this article in money, but also the rate of exchange between the two markets, or, in technical terms, between the two *places*, which may be respectively regarded as the commercial centres of the markets in question. For instance, if we take for our unit of value the value of one gram of silver in market A, the value of the commodity in market B, expressed in grams of silver, must be multiplied by the coefficient of exchange from A to B (Chapter III); and if this reduced value, added to the cost of transportation, gives a smaller sum than the value of the commodity in grams of silver in market A, then only will the transportation of the commodity from B to A take place.

It would be a complicated problem, and at the same time one of very little interest for economic theory, to determine the influence of the communication of markets on the price of an article which is the subject of a monopoly, as well in the importing as in the exporting market. It is easy to see that under any such hypothesis the effects of competition would be combined with those which result properly from the communication of markets; and it is simpler, as well as more important, to consider directly the case where the effects of monopoly are extinguished, *i.e.* where the production of the article in both markets is ruled by the laws of unlimited competition.

It is manifest in this case, as the production must always increase in the exporting market, that the price of the commodity will be higher there than before the outflow; and reciprocally, as the price must fall in the importing market, the quantity produced there will be smaller.

Before communication, the prices p_a, and p_b, in the two markets A and B were determined by equations of the form

$$\Omega_a\left(p_a\right) \;=\; F_a\left(p_a\right)$$
$$\Omega_b\left(p_b\right) \;=\; F_b\left(p_b\right) \tag{5.1}$$

in which the characteristics F and Ω have the signification which was attributed to them in Chapter VIII, and letters placed as indices at the foot of these characteristics serve to distinguish the functions which refer to market

A from those which are relative to market *B*.

After communication, these two equations are to be replaced by the following,

$$\Omega_a\left(p_a'\right) + \Omega_b\left(p_a' + \epsilon\right) = F_a\left(p_a'\right) + F_b\left(p_a' + \epsilon\right) \tag{5.2}$$

in which p_a' represents the price in the exporting market *A*, and ϵ the cost of transportation from *A* to *B*.

One of the interesting questions which can be proposed is to know whether the communication of markets always increases the total production, or, in other words analytically, whether we shall find in all cases

$$F_a\left(p_a'\right) + F_b\left(p_a' + \epsilon\right) > F_a\left(p_a\right) + F_b\left(p_b\right) \tag{5.3}$$

To settle this question in the negative, we have only to consider a particular case, which renders comparison of equations (5.1) and (5.2) more easy; namely, the case where the quantities p_a, p_b, and p_a' only vary by quantities so small that, for an approximate calculation, it is possible to neglect the squares and higher powers of these differences.

Let

$$p_a' = p_a + \delta \text{ and } p_a = p_a + \omega$$

whence, therefore,

$$p_a' + \epsilon = p_b + \delta + \epsilon - \omega$$

We must suppose $\omega > \epsilon$, as otherwise the establishment of communication would not determine a flow from *A* to *B*.

By applying to equation (5.2) the method of substitution, development, and reduction, of which we have already given many examples, this equation will become

$$\delta\left\{\Omega_a'\left(p_a\right) - F_a'\left(p_a\right)\right\} = \left(\delta + \epsilon - \omega\right)\left\{F_b'\left(p_b\right) - \Omega_b'\left(p_b\right)\right\} \tag{5.4}$$

and from the signs which are the essential characteristics of the functions F' and Ω' it is easy hence to deduce:

1. That δ is of the same sign as $\omega - \epsilon$, and consequently positive;

2. That we have $\delta < \omega - \epsilon$; which otherwise very evidently results from the fact that communication must raise the price of the commodity in the exporting market and depress it in the importing market.

Substituting now their values for p'_a and $p'_a + \epsilon$ in inequality (5.3), this becomes, after making the reductions,

$$\delta F'_a(p_a) + (\delta + \epsilon - \omega) F'_b(p_b) > 0$$

If from equation (5.4) we derive the value of $(\delta + \epsilon - \omega)$, and cancel the common factor δ, which is positive, the preceding inequality will become

$$F'_a(p_a) + \frac{F'_b(p_b)\{\Omega'_a(p_a) - F'_a(p_a)\}}{F'_b(p_b) - \Omega'_b(p_b)} > 0$$

or more simply, by eliminating the denominator, and changing the sign of the inequality because the denominator is negative,

$$F'_b(p_b)\Omega'_a(p_a) - F'_a(p_a)\Omega'_b(p_b) < 0$$

It is evident that this inequality, and consequently inequality (5.3), may or may not be satisfied according to the numerical relations of the functions F' and Ω'.

There is therefore no contradiction involved in admitting that the communication of markets diminishes the total production.

And, reciprocally, the isolation of markets may be a cause which increases the quantity of an article delivered for consumption. We intend here only to determine this fact, without pretending, which would be absurd, to contradict the opinion which has been very generally formed, of the advantages for the community procured by improvements in the means of communication or by the extension of markets. This question will be the subject of a thorough discussion further on.

It is well to remark that to make applicable the approximate formulas which we have just been using, it is not necessary that the quantities ω and ϵ should be very small with reference to the original prices p_a and p_b: it is enough that the differences δ and $\omega - \epsilon$ should be very small with reference to p_a.

5.2   J.S. Mill

This section contains material from J.S. Mill's 'great chapter' XVIII (1920, pp.583-597), from 1848, where he reproduces material previously published in 1844. He explores in detail the role of reciprocal demand and supply.

Of International Values

The values of commodities produced at the same place, or in places sufficiently adjacent for capital to move freely between them – let us say, for simplicity, of commodities produced in the same country – depend (temporary fluctuations apart) upon their cost of production. But the value of a commodity brought from a distant place, especially from a foreign country, does not depend on its cost of production in the place from whence it comes. On what, then, does it depend? The value of a thing in any place depends on the cost of its acquisition in that place; which, in the case of an imported article, means the cost of production of the thing which is exported to pay for it.

Since all trade is in reality barter, money being a mere instrument for exchanging things against one another, we will, for simplicity, begin by supposing the international trade to be in form, what it always is in reality, an actual trucking of one commodity against another. As far as we have hitherto proceeded, we have found all the laws of interchange to be essentially the same, whether money is used or not; money never governing, but always obeying, those general laws.

If, then, England imports wine from Spain, giving for every pipe of wine a bale of cloth, the exchange value of a pipe of wine in England will not depend upon what the production of the wine may have cost in Spain, but upon what the production of the cloth has cost in England. Though the wine may have cost in Spain the equivalent of only ten days' labour, yet, if the cloth costs in England twenty days' labour, the wine, when brought to England, will exchange for the produce of twenty days' English labour, plus the cost of carriage; including the usual profit on the importer's capital, during the time it is locked up, and withheld from other employment.

The value, then, in any country, of a foreign commodity, depends on the quantity of home produce which must be given to the foreign country in exchange for it. In other words, the values of foreign commodities depend on the terms of international exchange. What then, do these depend upon? What is it which, in the case supposed, causes a pipe of wine from Spain to be exchanged with England for exactly that quantity of cloth? We have seen that it is not their cost of production. If the cloth and the wine were both made in Spain, they would exchange at their cost of production in Spain; if they were both made in England, they would exchange at their cost of production in England: but all the cloth being made in England, and all the wine in Spain, they are in circumstances to which we have already determined that the law of cost of production is not applicable. We must accordingly, as we have done before in a similar embarrassment, fall back upon an antecedent law, that of supply and demand: and in this we shall again find the solution of our difficulty.

I have discussed this question in a separate Essay, already once referred to; and a quotation of part of the exposition then given will be the best introduction to my present view of the subject. I must give notice that we are now in the region of the most complicated questions which political economy affords; that the subject is one which cannot possibly be made elementary; and that a more continuous effort of attention than has yet been required will be necessary to follow the series of deductions. The thread however, which we are about to take in hand, is in itself very simple and manageable; the only difficulty is in following it through the windings and entanglements of complex international transactions.

When the trade is established between the two countries, the two commodities will exchange for each other at the same rate of interchange in both countries – bating the cost of carriage, of which, for the present, it will be more convenient to omit the consideration. Supposing, therefore, for the sake of argument, that the carriage of the commodities from one country to the other could be effected without labour and without cost, no sooner would the trade be opened than the value of the two commodities estimated in each other, would come to a level in both countries.

Suppose that 10 yards of broadcloth cost in England as much labour as 15 yards of linen, and in Germany as much as 20. In common with most of my predecessors, I find it advisable, in these intricate investigations, to give distinctness and fixity to the conception by numerical examples. These examples must sometimes, as in the present case, be purely supposititious. I should have preferred real ones; but all that is essential is, that the numbers should be such as admit of being easily followed through the subsequent combinations into which they enter.

This supposition then being made, it would be the interest of England to import linen from Germany, and of Germany to import cloth from England. When each country produced both commodities for itself, 10 yards of cloth exchanged for 15 yards of linen in England, and for 20 in Germany. They will now exchange for the same number of yards of linen in both. For what number? If for 15 yards, England will be just as she was, and Germany will gain all. If for 20 yards, Germany will be as before, and England will derive the whole of the benefit. If for any number intermediate between 15 and 20, the advantage will be shared between the two countries. If, for example, 10 yards of cloth exchange for 18 of linen, England will gain an advantage of 3 yards on every 15, Germany will save 2 out of every 20. The problem is, what are the causes which determine the proportion in which the cloth of England and the linen of Germany will exchange for each other.

As exchange value, in this case as in every other, is proverbially fluctuating, it does not matter what we suppose it to be when we begin: we shall soon see whether there be any fixed point above which it oscillates, which it has a tendency always to approach to, and to remain at. Let us suppose, then, that by the effect of what Adam Smith calls the higgling of the market, 10 yards of cloth in both countries exchange for 17 yards of linen.

The demand for a commodity, that is, the quantity of it which can find a purchaser, varies, as we have before remarked, according to the price. In Germany the price of 10 yards of cloth is now 17 yards of linen or whatever quantity of money is equivalent in Germany to 17 yards of linen. Now, that being the price, there is some particular number of yards of cloth, which will be in demand, or will find purchasers at that price. There is some given quantity of cloth, more than which could not be disposed of at that price, less than which, at that price, would not fully satisfy the demand. Let us suppose this quantity to be 1000 times 10 yards.

Let us now turn our attention to England. There, the price of 17 yards of linen is 10 yards of cloth, or whatever quantity of money is equivalent in England to 10 yards of cloth. There is some particular number of yards of linen which, at that price, will exactly satisfy demand, and no more. Let us suppose that this number is 1000 times 17 yards.

As 17 yards of linen are to 10 yards of cloth, so are 1000 times 17 yards to 1000 times 10 yards. At the existing exchange value, the linen which England requires will exactly pay for the quantity of cloth which, on the same terms of interchange Germany requires. The demand on each side is precisely sufficient to carry off the supply on the other. The conditions required by the principle of demand and supply are fulfilled, and the two commodities will continue to be interchanged, as we supposed them to be, in the ratio of 17 yards of linen for 10 yards of cloth.

But our suppositions might have been different. Suppose that at the assumed rate of interchange, England has been disposed to consume no greater quantity of linen than 800 times 17 yards: it is evident that, at the rate supposed, this would not have sufficed to pay for the 1000 times 10 yards of cloth which we have supposed Germany to require at the assumed value. Germany would be able to procure no more than 800 times 10 yards at that price. To procure the remaining 200, which she would have no means of doing but by bidding higher for them, she would offer more than 17 yards of linen in exchange for 10 yards of cloth: let us suppose her to offer 18. At this price, perhaps, England would be inclined to purchase a greater quantity of linen. She would consume, possibly, at that price, 900 times 18 yards. On the other hand, cloth having risen in price, the demand of Germany for it would probably have diminished. If, instead of 1000 times 10 yards, she is now contented with 900 times 10 yards, these will exactly pay for the 900 times 18 yards of linen which England is willing to take at the altered price: the demand on each side will again exactly suffice to take off the corresponding supply and 10 yards for 18 will be the rate at which, in both countries, cloth will exchange for linen.

The converse of all this would have happened, if, instead of 800 times 17 yards, we had supposed that England, at the rate of 10 for 17, would have taken 1200 times 17 yards of linen. In this case, it is England whose demand is not fully supplied; it is England who, by bidding for more linen, will alter the rate of interchange to her own disadvantage; and 10 yards of cloth will fall, in both countries, below the value of 17 yards of linen. By this fall of cloth, or, what is the same thing this rise of linen, the demand of Germany for cloth will increase, and the demand of England for linen will diminish, till the rate of interchange has so adjusted itself that the cloth and the linen will exactly pay for one another; and when once this point is attained, values will remain without further alteration.

It may be considered, therefore, as established, that when two countries trade together in two commodities, the exchange value of these commodities relatively to each other will adjust itself to the inclinations and circumstances of the consumers on both sides, in such manner that the quantities required by each country, of the articles which it imports from its neighbour, shall be exactly sufficient to pay for one another. As the inclinations and circumstances of consumers cannot be reduced to any rule, so neither can the proportions in which the two commodities will be interchanged. We know that the limits, within which the variation is confined, are the ratio between their costs of production in the one country and the ratio between their costs of production in the other. Ten yards of cloth cannot exchange for more than 20 yards of linen, nor for less than 15. But they may exchange for any intermediate number. The ratios, therefore, in which the advantage of the trade may be divided between the two nations are various. The circumstances on which the proportionate share of each country more remotely depends, admit only of a very general indication.

It is even possible to conceive an extreme case, in which the whole of the advantage resulting from the interchange would be reaped by one party, the other country gaining nothing at all. There is no absurdity in the hypothesis that, of some given commodity, a certain quantity is all that is wanted at any price; and that, when that quantity is obtained, no fall in the exchange value would induce other consumers to come forward, or those who are already supplied to take more. Let us suppose that this is the case in Germany with cloth. Before her trade with England commenced, when 10 yards of cloth cost her as much labour as 20 yards of linen, she nevertheless consumed as much cloth as she wanted under any circumstances, and, if she could obtain it at the rate of 10 yards of cloth for 15 of linen, she would not consume more. Let this fixed quantity be 1000 times 10 yards. At the rate, however, of 10 for 20, England would want more linen than would be equivalent to this quantity of cloth. She would, consequently, offer a higher value for linen; or, what is the same thing, she would offer her cloth at a cheaper rate. But, as by no lowering of the value could she prevail on Germany to take a greater quantity of cloth, there would be no limit to the rise of linen or fall of cloth, until the demand of England for linen was reduced by the rise of its value, to the quantity which 1000 times 10 yards of cloth would purchase. It might be, that to produce this diminution of the demand a less fall would not suffice than that which would make 10 yards of cloth exchange for 16 of linen. Germany would then gain the whole of the advantage, and England would be exactly as she was before the trade commenced. It would be for the interest, however, of Germany herself to keep her linen a little below the value at which it could be produced in England, in order to keep herself from being supplanted by the home producer. England, therefore, would always benefit in some degree by the existence of the trade, though it might be a very trifling one.

In this statement, I conceive, is contained the first elementary principle of International Values. I have, as is indispensable in such abstract and hypothetical cases, supposed the circumstances to be much less complex than they really are: in the first place, by suppressing the cost of carriage; next, by supposing that there are only two countries trading together; and lastly, that they trade only in two commodities. To render the exposition of the principle complete it is necessary to restore the various circumstances thus temporarily left out to simplify the argument. Those who are accustomed to any kind of scientific investigation will probably see, without formal proof, that the introduction of these circumstances cannot alter the theory of the

subject. Trade among any number of countries, and in any number of commodities, must take place on the same essential principles as trade between
two countries and in two commodities. Introducing a greater number of
agents precisely similar cannot change the law of their action, no more than
putting additional weights into the two scales of a balance alters the law of
gravitation. It alters nothing but the numerical results. For more complete
satisfaction, however, we will enter into the complex cases with the same
particularity with which we have stated the simpler one.

First, let us introduce the element of cost of carriage ... It is impossible
to say, if the cost of carriage could be annihilated, whether the producing or
the importing country would be most benefited. This would depend on the
play of international demand.

Let us now introduce a greater number of commodities than the two we
have hitherto supposed ... If, therefore, it be asked what country draws to
itself the greatest share of the advantage of any trade it carries on, the answer
is, the country for whose productions there is in other countries the greatest
demand, and a demand the most susceptible of increase from additional
cheapness. In so far as the productions of any country possess this property,
the country obtains all foreign commodities at less cost. It sets its imports
cheaper, the greater the intensity of the demand in foreign countries for its
exports. It also gets its imports cheaper, the less the extent and intensity of
its own demand for them. The market is cheapest to those whose demand is
small. A country which desires few foreign productions, and only a limited
quantity of them, while its own commodities are in great request in foreign
countries, will obtain its limited imports at extremely small cost, that is, in
exchange for the produce of a very small quantity of its labour and capital.

Lastly, having introduced more than the original two commodities into
the hypothesis let us also introduce more than the original two countries ...
It deserves notice, that this effect in favour of England from the opening of
another market for her exports, will equally be produced even though the
country from which the demand comes should have nothing to sell which
England is willing to take. Suppose that the third country, though requiring
cloth or iron from England, produces no linen, nor any other article which

is in demand there ... Everything will take place precisely as if the third country had bought German produce with her own goods, and offered that produce to England in exchange for hers. There is an increased demand for English goods, for which German goods have to furnish the payment; and this can only be done by forcing an increased demand for them in England, that is, by lowering their value. Thus an increase of demand for a country's exports in any foreign country enables her to obtain more cheaply even those imports which she procures from other quarters. And conversely, an increase of her own demand for any foreign commodity compels her, *ceteris paribus*, to pay dearer for all foreign commodities.

The law which we have now illustrated, may be appropriately named, the Equation of International Demand. It may be concisely stated as follows. The produce of a country exchanges for the produce of other countries, at such values as are required in order that the whole of her exports may exactly pay for the whole of her imports. This law of International Values is but an extension of the more general law of Value, which we called the Equation of Supply and Demand. We have seen that the value of a commodity always so adjusts itself as to bring the demand to the exact level of the supply.

But all trade, either between nations or individuals, is an interchange of commodities, in which the things that they respectively have to sell constitute also their means of purchase: the supply brought by the one constitutes his demand for what is brought by the other. So that supply and demand are but another expression for reciprocal demand: and to say that value will adjust itself so as to equalize demand with supply, is in fact to say that it will adjust itself so as to equalize the demand on one side with the demand on the other.

To trace the consequences of this law of International Values through their wide ramifications, would occupy more space than can be here devoted to such a purpose ... Suppose now a change in that cost of production; an improvement, for example, in the process of manufacture. Will the benefit of the improvement be fully participated in by other countries? Will the commodity be sold as much cheaper to foreigners, as it is produced cheaper at home? This question, and the considerations which must be entered into in order to resolve it, are well adapted to try the worth of the theory. ...

Of the three possible varieties in the influence of cheapness on demand, which is the more probable – that the demand would be increased more than the cheapness, as much as the cheapness, or less than the cheapness? This depends on the nature of the particular commodity, and on the tastes of purchasers. When the commodity is one in general request, and the fall of its price brings it within reach of a much larger class of incomes than before, the demand is often increased in a greater ratio than the fall of price, and a larger sum of money is on the whole expended in the article. Such was the case with coffee, when its price was lowered by successive reductions of taxation; and such would probably be the case with sugar, wine, and a large class of commodities which, though not necessaries, are largely consumed, and in which many consumers indulge when the articles are cheap and economize when they are dear. But it more frequently happens that when a commodity falls in price, less money is spent in it than before: a greater quantity is consumed, but not so great a value. The consumer who saves more by the cheapness of the article, will be likely to expend part of the saving in increasing his consumption of other things: and unless the low price attracts a large class of new purchasers who were either not customers of the article at all, or only in small quantity and occasionally, a less aggregate sum will be expended on it. Speaking generally, therefore, the third of our three cases is the most probable and an improvement in an exportable article is likely to be as beneficial (if not more beneficial) to foreign countries, as to the country where the article is produced.

Thus far had the theory of international values been carried in the first and second editions of this work. But intelligent criticisms (chiefly those of my friend Mr. William Thornton), and subsequent further investigation, have shown that the doctrine stated in the preceding pages, though correct as far as it goes, is not yet the complete theory of the subject matter.

It has been shown that the exports and imports between the two countries (or, if we suppose more than two, between each country and the world) must in the aggregate pay for each other, and must therefore be exchanged for one another at such values as will be compatible with the equation of international demand. That this, however, does not furnish the complete law of the phenomenon, appears from the following consideration: that several different rates of international value may all equally fulfil the conditions of this law ... There is still therefore a portion of indeterminateness in the rate at which the international values would adjust themselves; showing that the whole of the influencing circumstances cannot yet have been taken into account.

5.3   Whewell

This section contains Whewell's (1850, pp.10-13) international trade model, inspired by Mill's analysis. Here he makes use of his specification of demand functions using the 'specific rate of change'; see chapter 4 above.

Some Doctrines of Political Economy

The preceding formulae apply to prices as affected by demand and production within the limits of our country. Prices within such a circle are governed ultimately by the cost of production. The prices of unit of each of two commodities C and D, are as the cost of production of the two; that is, as the labour (including skill estimated in labour) by which each is produced and brought to market. For if the ratio of the prices were different from this, labour would be transferred from the production of the one to that of the other, so as to tend to restore the equality. But between foreign countries there is no such tendency to equilibrium between price and labour, because labour is not transferred from one country to another when the prices are in different ratio. A pound of tea, if produced in China by the same labour which produces a yard of cloth in England, may nevertheless exchange for two yards, or for half a yard for there will not be a transfer of tea-producing labour to produce cloth, in the first case, or of cloth-producing labour to tea in the second. Hence then the relation of prices of commodities, native and imported, is not governed by the equations already given. By what then is it governed? What is the principle which regulates *international values*? (Mill, *Polit. Econ.* II. 121)

The principle which regulates such values is (in addition to the principle of supply and demand already spoken of) this: that when the international trade has been established, the relative value of all commodities which are exported and imported is the same in the two countries (omitting for the present the cost of carriage). This we may call *the principle of uniformity of international prices.* It is evident that if tea and cloth are exchanged between China and England, the rate of exchange of the two must be the same in the two countries: for if it were not, the current of trade would be determined one way or other, and would, by increasing the import of the one commodity or the other, tend to restore the equilibrium.

In order to apply this principle, let there be two commodities (C) and (D) (cloth and linen for example) and let C and D represent the value of a unit (yard) of each in terms of any other commodity.

Suppose that in England p is the price of D in terms of C; and let q be the quantity of (D) consumed (that is bought) in England at that price.

Then $D = pC, C = \frac{D}{p}$ in England.

Suppose that in Germany P is the price of C in terms of D, and let Q be the quantity of (C) consumed in Germany at that price.

Then $C = PD, D = \frac{C}{P}$ in Germany.

Now D in England costs pC when there is no international trade; but if obtained from Germany by exporting C, would there cost $\frac{C}{P}$.

Therefore there would be a gain for England in obtaining D by exporting C rather than producing it at home if $pC > \frac{C}{P}$; that is, if $Pp > 1$: for the cost would be less.

In like manner, there would be a gain for Germany in obtaining C by exporting D rather than by producing it at home, if $PD > \frac{D}{p}$; that is, if $P_p > 1$: for the cost would be less.

Hence on the supposition that England exports C and imports D, and Germany exports D and imports C, both countries gain.

What will be the amount of the exports and imports, and the prices, when the international trade exists?

In order to solve this problem, we must introduce another principle; namely this: that in the long run, and in the permanent condition of the trade, the value of the exports of each country must equal the value of its imports. For each country pays for its imports by its exports.

Under the trade let p, the price of D in terms of C, in England, become p'; and q, the quantity of (D) consumed in England, become q', the whole being imported from Germany. And let P, the price of C in terms of D in Germany become P', and let Q, the quantity of (C) consumed in Germany, become Q', the whole being imported from England.

In England $p'C = D$, in Germany, $P'D = C$; and since these equations express prices under the trade, by the principle of uniformity of international prices, the relation of C and D is the same in the two countries. Therefore multiplying together the two equations,

$$P'p' = 1$$

which is the *equation of uniformity of international prices*.

England exports Q' of (C) and imports q' of (D); and of this last the value is $p'q'$ in terms of C: therefore ... $p'q' = Q'$.

In the same manner Germany exports q' of (D) and imports Q' of (C); and of this last the value is $P'Q'$ in terms of D: therefore $P'Q' = q'$.

The equation $p'q' = Q'$, or $P'Q' = q'$ is *the equation of import and export*. The two equations are identical in virtue of the equation $P'p' = 1$.

Now to find the quantities of the imports and the prices.

The consumption of (D) in England varies with the price. When the price falls from pC to $p'C$, let the quantity consumed be increased from q to q'. Let $p' = p(1 - x)$, and let the law of altered money demand be, as before, $p'q' = pq(1 - mx)$. Hence $q' = q\frac{1-mx}{1-x}$.

In like manner the demand for (C) in Germany varies with the price. Let $P' = P(1 - X)$, $P'Q' = PQ(1 - MX)$; whence $Q' = Q\frac{1-MX}{1-X}$.

Since $p(1 - x) = p'$, $P(1 - X) = P'$, we have $Pp(1 - X)(1 - x) = P'p' = 1$.

Hence $(1 - X)(1 - x) = \frac{1}{Pp} = 1 - k$, suppose, k being a fraction; since $...Pp$ is greater than 1.

The equation $(1 - X)(1 - x) = 1 - k$, gives $X = \frac{k-x}{1-x}$.

The equation $q' = P'Q'$, (37), gives $q\frac{1-mx}{1-x} = PQ(1 - MX)$.

Put for X its value $\frac{k-x}{1-x}$, and solve the equation in x; and we find

$$x = \frac{PQ\,(1 - Mk) - q}{PQ\,(1 - M) - mq}$$

The values of x and X depend upon the ratio existing between PQ and q originally, before the trade: that is, upon the relative value of (C) consumed in Germany and of (D) consumed in England and also upon m and M, the specific rate of change of each commodity.

In general let $PQ = nq$; and we have

$$x = \frac{n\,(1 - Mk) - 1}{n\,(1 - M) - m} \text{ or } x = \frac{1 - n\,(1 - Mk)}{m - n\,(1 - M)}$$

I will apply these formulae to the numerical examples given by Mr. Mill, (*Polit. Econ.* II. 123). ...

Chapter 6

Formal Exchange Models

This chapter begins with three examples of early treatments of exchange, before moving to the more formal models of Jevons and Walras.

6.1 Cantillon

This section contains material from chapter II of Cantillon (1931, pp.117-121), dating from 1755, where he discusses the determination of market prices.

Of Market Prices

Suppose the Butchers on one side and the Buyers on the other. The price of Meat will be settled after some altercations, and a pound of Beef will be in value to a piece of silver pretty nearly as the whole Beef offered for sale in the Market is to all the silver brought there to buy Beef.

This proportion is come at by bargaining. The Butcher keeps up his Price according to the number of Buyers he sees; the Buyers, on their side, offer less according as they think the Butcher will have less sale: the Price set by some is usually followed by others. Some are more clever in puffing up their wares, others in running them down. Though this method of fixing Market prices has no exact or geometrical foundation, since it often depends upon the eagerness or easy temperament of a few Buyers or Sellers, it does not seem that it could be done in any more convenient way. It is clear that the quantity of Produce or of Merchandise offered for sale, in proportion to the demand or number of Buyers, is the basis on which is fixed or always supposed to be fixed the actual Market Prices; and that in general these prices do not vary much from the intrinsic value.

Let us take another case. Several maîtres d'hôtels have been told to buy green Peas when they first come in. One Master has ordered the purchase of 10 quarts for 60 livres, another 10 quarts for 50 livres, a third 10 for 40 livres, and a fourth 10 for 30 livres. If these orders are to be carried out there must be 40 quarts of green Peas in the Market. Suppose there are only 20. The Vendors, seeing many Buyers, will keep up their Prices, and the Buyers will come up to the Prices prescribed to them: so that those who offer 60 livres for 10 quarts will be the first served. The Sellers, seeing later that no one will go above 50, will let the other 10 quarts go at that price. Those who had orders not to exceed 40 and 30 livres will go away empty.

If instead of 40 quarts there were 400, not only would the Maîtres d'hôtels get the new Peas much below the sums laid down for them, but the Sellers in order to be preferred one to the other by the few Buyers will lower their new Peas almost to their intrinsic value, and in that case many Maîtres d'Hôtels who had no orders will buy some.

It often happens that Sellers who are too obstinate in keeping up their price in the Market, miss the opportunity of selling their Produce or Merchandise to advantage and are losers thereby. It also happens that by sticking to their prices they may be able to sell more profitably another day.

Distant Markets may always affect the prices of the Market where one is: if corn is extremely dear in France it will go up in England and in other neighbouring Countries.

6.2   Turgot

This section contains material from Turgot (1973, pp.90-94), dating from the late 1760s, where he examines the determination of values in an exchange framework.

Value and Money

Let us take up the thread of the argument which has led us to where we now are; let us extend our first assumption. Instead of considering only one man in isolation, let us gather two men together: let each have in his possession certain things suitable for his use, but let these things be different and adapted to different needs. Let us suppose, for example, that two savages land separately on a desert island in the northern seas. One of them brings with him in his boat more fish than he can consume; the other brings more skins than he can use to clothe himself and make himself a tent. The one who has brought fish is cold, and the one who has brought skins is hungry; what will happen is that the latter will ask the possessor of the fish for a part of his supply, and will offer to give him in its place some of his skins: the other will accept. Here we have exchange, here we have trade.

Let us stop for a moment to consider what happens in this exchange. It is clear, first, that the man who, after having taken out of his catch the amount necessary for his subsistence for a small number of days beyond which the fish would go bad, would have thrown the remainder away as useless, begins to set store by them when he sees that these fish can serve to procure for him (by way of exchange) the skins which he needs in order to clothe himself; this surplus of fish acquires in his eyes a value which it did not formerly have. The possessor of skins will reason in the same way, and will learn for his part to *evaluate* those for which he does not have a *personal* need. It is probable that in this first situation, where we assume that each of our two men is superabundantly provided with the thing he possesses, and is not accustomed to attach any price to the surplus, the discussion about the conditions of the exchange will not be a very lively one; each will allow the other to take in the one case all the fish and in the other all the skins which he himself does not need. But let us change the assumption a little: let us give to each of these two men an interest in keeping his surplus, a motive for attaching value to it: let us assume that instead of fish one of them has brought maize, which will keep for a very long time; that the other instead of skins has brought firewood, and that the island produces neither corn nor wood. One of our two savages has his subsistence, and the other his heating, for several months; they can go and renew their supplies only by returning to the mainland, from which they have perhaps been driven by the fear of wild beasts or a hostile nation; they can do it only by exposing themselves on the sea, in a stormy season, to almost inevitable dangers. Under these circumstances, it is clear that the total quantity of maize and the total quantity of wood will become very precious to their two possessors, and that they will regard them as having a considerable value; but the wood which the one could consume in a month would become completely useless to him if he died of hunger in the meantime through lack of maize, and the possessor of maize would not be any more advantaged if he were exposed to the risk of dying of cold through lack of wood. Thus they will once again make an exchange, in order that they should both have enough wood and maize to last them until the weather or the season allowed them to go to sea in order to search on the mainland for more maize and more wood. In this situation both will no doubt be less generous; each will very carefully weigh up all the considerations which may induce him to prefer a certain quantity of the good which he does not possess to a certain quantity of that which he does; that is, he will calculate the strength of the two needs, the two interests which he is balancing one against the other—namely, the interest in keeping maize and in acquiring wood and that in acquiring maize and keeping wood. In a word, he will determine very precisely their *esteem value* relative to himself. This *esteem value* is proportionate to the *interest* which he has in procuring these two things, and the comparison of the two *values* is clearly nothing but the comparison of the two *interests*. But each one makes this calculation separately, and the results may be different: one would exchange three measures of maize for six armfuls of wood; the other would only be willing to give his six armfuls of wood for nine measures of maize. Independently of this kind of mental evaluation in which each man compares the interest which he has in keeping to that which he has in acquiring, both of them are also impelled by an interest which is general and independent of all comparisons: that is, the interest which each one has in keeping as much as he can of his own good and acquiring as much as he can of the other's good. Having this in view, each one will keep secret the comparison he has inwardly made of his two interests, the two values which he attaches to the two goods which are to be exchanged, and he will sound out the possessor of the good which he desires by making smaller offers and larger demands. The latter will behave for his part in the same way, and they will argue about the conditions of the exchange; and, since they both have a great interest in reaching agreement, they will in the end agree. Little by little, each of them will increase his offers or reduce his demands, until they finally settle that a determinate quantity of maize should be given for a determinate quantity of wood. At the moment when the exchange is made, the one who gives, for example, four measures of maize for five armfuls of wood, no doubt prefers these five armfuls to the four measures of maize; he affords them a higher esteem value; but the one who receives the four measures of maize for his part prefers them to the five armfuls of wood. This superiority of the *esteem value* attributed by the acquirer to the thing which is acquired over the thing which is given up, is essential to exchange, since it is the sole motive for it. Everyone would stay as he was if he did not find an interest, a personal profit, in exchanging – if, relative to himself, he did not esteem what he received more highly than what he gave.

But this difference in esteem value is reciprocal and exactly equal on each side; for, if it were not equal, one of the two would have less desire for the exchange and would force the other to come nearer to his price by means of a higher offer. Thus it is always strictly true that each gives equal value in order to receive *equal value*. If four measures of corn are given for five armfuls of wood, then five armfuls of wood are also given for four measures of maize, and consequently four measures of maize *are equivalent*, in this particular exchange, to five armfuls of wood. Thus these two things have an equal exchange value.

Let us stop once again. Let us see what exactly is meant by this exchange value, the equality of which is the necessary condition of a free exchange; let us not yet depart at all from the simplicity of our hypothesis, in which we have only two contracting parties and two objects of exchange to be considered. It is not exactly the *esteem value*, or, in other words, the interest which each of the two men attached separately to the two objects of need, the possession of which he compared in order to determine what he ought to give up of the one in order to acquire the other, since the result of this comparison could be unequal in the minds of the two contracting parties. This first value, to which we have given the name *esteem value*, is established through the comparison which each of the men separately makes between the two interests which contend with one another in his case; it has no existence except in the mind of each of them taken separately. Exchange value, on the other hand, is adopted by both the contracting parties, who acknowledge its equality and make it the condition of the exchange. In the determination of *esteem value*, each man, taken separately, has compared only two interests: the two interests which he attaches to the object which he has and to the object which he desires to have. In the determination of *exchange value*, there are two men who are comparing and there are four interests which are compared; but the two individual interests of each of the two contracting parties have at first been compared with one another separately, and it is the two results which are subsequently compared with one another, or rather argued about, by the two contracting parties, in order to form an *average esteem value* which becomes precisely the *exchange value*, and to which I believe we should give the name *appraisal value*, because it determines the price or the condition of the exchange.

We can see from what has just been said that the *appraisal value* – that value which is equal as between the two objects exchanged – is essentially of the same nature as the esteem value; it differs from it only because it is an *average esteem value*. We have seen above that for each of the contracting parties the *esteem value* of the thing which is received is higher than that of the thing which is given, and that this difference is exactly equal on each side; by taking one-half of this difference in order to subtract it from the higher value and add it to the lower, we will make them *equal*. We have seen that this perfect equality is precisely the characteristic of the *appraisal value* of the exchange. This *appraisal value*, therefore, is clearly nothing else but the *average of the esteem values* which the two contracting parties attach to each object.

We have proved that the *esteem value* of an object, for a man in isolation, is nothing else but the relation between the portion of his resources which a man can devote to the search for that object and the totality of his resources; thus the appraisal value in the exchange between two men is the relation between the sum of the portions of their respective resources which they would be disposed to devote to the search for each of the objects exchanged and the sum of the resources of these two men.

It is worth noting here that the introduction of exchange between our two men increases the wealth of both – that is, it gives them a greater quantity of enjoyments with the same resources. Let us assume, in the example of our two savages, that the area which produces the maize and that which produces the wood are far distant from one another. One savage on his own would be obliged to make two voyages to get his supply of maize and his supply of wood; thus he would expend a great deal of time and effort in sailing. If on the other hand there are two of them, they will employ, one in cutting wood and the other in procuring maize, the time and labour which making the second voyage would have involved them in. The sum total of maize and wood gathered in will be greater, and so, consequently, will be the share of each man.

6.3   Hearn

This section contains material from chapter XIV of Hearn (1863, pp.235-237) where he examines the important role of exchange in economics.

Of Exchange

I now approach the consideration of that great agent which with an excusable exaggeration some writers have regarded as the sole subject of economic science. Although a less exalted rank has been assigned in these pages to the theory of exchange, this lower view of its position does not proceed from any insensibility to its influence. Coming into at least full operation at a late period of industrial development, exchange quickens into new life as well the primary elements of production as its own fellow industrial auxiliaries. It suggests to the labourer new wants. It at the same time provides the easiest means of satisfying these wants. It enables the ignorant and the weak innocently to profit by the learning of the wise, and the vigour of the strong. It extends to the inhabitants of different regions a share in those natural advantages of which nature seems to have granted to each region the exclusive possession. It affords larger means for the accumulation of capital, and an ampler field for its profitable occupation. To its demands for increased facilities both of production and of intercourse some of our most important inventions are due. Above all, it is the complement and the crown of cooperation, carrying out the full effects of that great auxiliary to an extent that would otherwise be impracticable, and establishing not only between unacquainted individuals but remote and jealous nations an unpremeditated and almost unconscious, yet not the less complete or effectual, system of association. Nor must we omit, although they hardly come within the range of the present inquiry the indirect benefits of exchange. It enlarges the sphere of men's observation and so of their knowledge. It substitutes for the ferocious antipathies of an earlier age the friendly relations which spring from a sense of reciprocal advantage. It renders both parties dependent on each other for a multitude of their daily enjoyments, and thus binds them in a sort of unacknowledged yet powerful frankpledge. Disputes consequently whether private or national tend to become more odious in conception and less facile in execution. Thus by a method that the most obtuse cannot overlook, and the most wilful cannot misunderstand, it teaches the great moral lesson that the benefit of each is the benefit of all; and that a wrong done to one class is sure to extend its influence over the whole community.

Exchange may be described as the voluntary transfer by one person to another of one instrument of enjoyment in consideration of the reciprocal transfer of a different one. There must therefore be two parties to every exchange; and there must also be a consideration. It is this latter circumstance which distinguishes exchange from other forms of giving, and receiving. A free gift is something different from all exchange: so is a robbery: so too is a tribute. All these transactions fail in the essential condition of reciprocity. There is no *quid pro quo*. But as in an exchange there is something received, so also there is something given. There are two parties, each of whom is influenced by the desire of enjoyment and the dislike of effort; and to each of whom the transaction presents itself in a different light. Each has an inducement and a sacrifice; but the inducement and the sacrifice are reciprocally inverted. Each obtains at a smaller cost than he otherwise could the means of satisfying a desire or of accomplishing a purpose: and each therefore finds, or expects that he will find, the exchange beneficial. From these considerations the conditions of exchange may be deduced. In every such transaction there must be enjoyment, and in like manner there must be cost. There must also be a proportion between that enjoyment and that cost; and that proportion must be more or less in favour of the enjoyment. Further, as there are two parties to every exchange, the principles now stated must apply equally to each of the two, and therefore the transaction must be, at least in their opinion at that time, beneficial to each.

6.4   Jevons

This section contains material from chapter IV of Jevons (1957, pp.88-101; 115-119; 142-145), first published in 1871, where he provides his central analysis of exchange.

The Theory of Political Economy
Definition of Trading Body

I find it necessary to adopt some expression for any number of people whose aggregate influence in a market, either in the way of supply or demand, we have to consider. By a *trading body* I mean, in the most general manner, any body either of buyers or sellers. The trading body may be a single individual in one case; it may be the whole inhabitants of a continent in another; it may be the individuals of a trade diffused through a country in a third. England and North America will be trading bodies if we are considering the corn we receive from America in exchange for iron and other goods. The continent of Europe is a trading body as purchasing coal from England. The farmers of England are a trading body when they sell corn to the millers, and the millers both when they buy corn from the farmers and sell flour to the bakers.

We must use the expression with this wide meaning, because the principles of exchange are the same in nature, however wide or narrow may be the market considered. Every trading body is either an individual or an aggregate of individuals, and the law, in the case of the aggregate, must depend upon the fulfilment of law in the individuals. We cannot usually observe any precise and continuous variation in the wants and deeds of an individual, because the action of extraneous motives, or what would seem to be caprice, overwhelms minute tendencies. As I have already remarked ... a single individual does not vary his consumption of sugar, butter, or eggs from week to week by infinitesimal amounts, according to each small change in the price. He probably continues his ordinary consumption until accident directs his attention to a rise in price, and he then, perhaps, discontinues the use of the articles altogether for a time. But the aggregate, or what is the same, the average consumption, of a large community will be found to vary continuously or nearly so. The most minute tendencies make themselves apparent in a wide average. Thus, our laws of Economics will be theoretically true in the case of individuals, and practically true in the case of large aggregates; but the general principles will be the same, whatever the extent of the trading body considered. We shall be justified, then, in using the expression with the utmost generality.

It should be remarked, however, that the economic laws representing the conduct of large aggregates of individuals will never represent exactly the conduct of any one individual. If we could imagine that there were a thousand individuals all exactly alike in regard to their demand for commodities, and their capabilities of supplying them, then the average laws of supply and demand deduced from the conduct of such individuals would agree with the conduct of any one individual. But a community is composed of persons differing widely in their powers, wants, habits, and possessions. In such circumstances the average laws applying to them will come under what I have elsewhere called the 'Fictitious Mean', that is to say, they are numerical results which do not pretend to represent the character of any existing thing. But average laws would not on this account be less useful, if we could obtain them; for the movements of trade and industry depend upon averages and aggregates, not upon the whims of individuals.

The Law of Indifference

When a commodity is perfectly uniform or homogeneous in quality any portion may be indifferently used in place of an equal portion: hence, in the same market, and at the same moment, all portions must be exchanged at the same ratio. There can be no reason why a person should treat exactly similar things differently, and the slightest excess in what is demanded for one over the other will cause him to take the latter instead of the former. In nicely balanced exchanges it is a very minute scruple which turns the scale and governs the choice. A minute difference of quality in a commodity may thus give rise to preference, and cause the ratio of exchange to differ. But where no difference exists at all, or where no difference is known to exist, there can be no ground for preference whatever. If, in selling a quantity of perfectly equal and uniform barrels of flour, a merchant arbitrarily fixed different prices on them, a purchaser would of course select the cheaper ones; and where there was absolutely no difference in the thing purchased, even an excess of a penny in the price of a thing worth a thousand pounds would be a valid ground of choice. Hence follows what is undoubtedly true, with proper explanations, that *in the same open market, at any one moment, there cannot be two prices for the same kind of article.* Such differences as may practically occur arise from extraneous circumstances, such as the defective credit of the purchasers, their imperfect knowledge of the market, and so on.

The principle above expressed is a general law of the utmost importance in Economics, and I propose to call it *The Law of Indifference,* meaning that, when two objects or commodities are subject to no important difference as regards the purpose in view, they will either of them be taken instead of the other with perfect indifference by a purchaser. Every such act of indifferent choice gives rise to an equation of degrees of utility, so that in this principle of indifference we have one of the central pivots of the theory.

Though the price of the same commodity must be uniform at any one moment, it may vary from moment to moment, and must be conceived as in a state of continual change. Theoretically speaking, it would not usually be possible to buy two portions of the same commodity *successively* at the same ratio of exchange, because, no sooner would the first portion have been bought than the conditions of utility would be altered. When exchanges are made on a large scale, this result will be verified in practice.[1] If a wealthy person invested £100, 000 in the funds in the morning, it is hardly likely that the operation could be repeated in the afternoon at the same price. In any market, if a person goes on buying largely, he will ultimately raise the price

---

[1]It is, I believe, verified in the New York Stock Markets, where it is the practice to sell Stocks by auction in successive lots, without disclosing the total amount to be put up. When the amount offered begins to exceed what was expected, then each successive lot brings a less price, and those who bought the earlier lots suffer. But if the amount offered is small, the early buyers have the advantage. Such an auction sale only exhibits in miniature what is constantly going on in the markets generally on a large scale.

against himself. Thus it is apparent that extensive purchases would best be made gradually, so as to secure the advantage of a lower price upon the earlier portions. In theory this effect of exchange upon the ratio of exchange must be conceived to exist in some degree, however small may be the purchases made. Strictly speaking, the ratio of exchange at any moment is that of dy to dx, of an infinitely small quantity of one commodity to the infinitely small quantity of another which is given for it. The ratio of exchange is really a differential coefficient. The quantity of any article purchased is a function of the price at which it is purchased, and the ratio of exchange expresses the rate at which the quantity of the article increases compared with what is given for it.

We must carefully distinguish, at the same time, between the Statics and Dynamics of this subject. The real condition of industry is one of perpetual motion and change. Commodities are being continually manufactured and exchanged and consumed. If we wished to have a complete solution of the problem in all its natural complexity, we should have to treat it as a problem of motion – a problem of dynamics. But it would surely be absurd to attempt the more difficult question when the more easy one is yet so imperfectly within our power. It is only as a purely statical problem that I can venture to treat the action of exchange. Holders of commodities will be regarded not as continuously passing on these commodities in streams of trade, but as possessing certain fixed amounts which they exchange until they come to equilibrium.

It is much more easy to determine the point at which a pendulum will come to rest than to calculate the velocity at which it will move when displaced from that point of rest. Just so, it is a far more easy task to lay down the conditions under which trade is completed and interchange ceases, than to attempt to ascertain at what rate trade will go on when equilibrium is not attained.

The difference will present itself in this form: dynamically we could not treat the ratio of exchange otherwise than as the ratio of dy and dx, infinitesimal quantities of commodity. Our equations would then be regarded as differential equations, which would have to be integrated. But in the statical view of the question we can substitute the ratio of the finite quantities y and x. Thus, from the self-evident principle ... that there cannot, in the same market, at the same moment, be two different prices for the same uniform commodity, it follows that *the last increments in an act of exchange must be exchanged in the same ratio as the whole quantities exchanged.* Suppose that two commodities are bartered in the ratio of x for y; then every m^{th} part of x is given for the mth part of y, and it does not matter for which of the mth parts. No part of the commodity can be treated differently from any other part. We may carry this division to an indefinite extent by imagining m to be constantly increased, so that, at the limit, even an infinitely small part of x must be exchanged for an infinitely small part of y, in the same ratio as the whole quantities. This result we may express by stating that the increments concerned in the process of exchange must obey the equation

$$\frac{dy}{dx} = \frac{y}{x} \tag{6.1}$$

The use which we shall make of this equation will be seen in the next section.

The Theory of Exchange

The keystone of the whole Theory of Exchange, and of the principal problems of Economics, lies in this proposition – *The ratio of exchange of any two commodities will be the reciprocal of the ratio of the final degrees of utility of the quantities of commodity available for consumption after the exchange is completed.* When the reader has reflected a little upon the meaning of this proposition, he will see, I think, that it is necessarily true, if the principle of human nature have been correctly represented in previous pages.

Imagine that there is one trading body possessing only corn, and another possessing only beef. It is certain that, under these circumstances, a portion of the corn may be given in exchange for a portion of the beef with a considerable increase of utility. How are we to determine at what point the exchange will cease to be beneficial? This question must involve both the ratio of exchange and the degrees of utility. Suppose, for a moment, that the ratio of exchange is approximately that of ten pounds of corn for one pound of beef: then if, to the trading body which possesses corn, ten pounds of corn are less useful than one of beef, that body will desire to carry the exchange further. Should the other body possessing beef find one pound less useful than ten pounds of corn, this body will also be desirous to continue the exchange. Exchange will thus go on until each party has obtained all the benefit that is possible, and loss of utility would result if more were exchanged. Both parties, then, rest in satisfaction and equilibrium, and the degrees of utility have come to their level, as it were.

This point of equilibrium will be known by the criterion, that an infinitely small amount of commodity exchanged in addition, at the same rate, will bring neither gain nor loss of utility. In other words, if increments of commodities be exchanged at the established ratio, their utilities will be equal for both parties. Thus, if ten pounds of corn were of exactly the same utility as one pound of beef, there would be neither harm nor good in further exchange at this ratio.

It is hardly possible to represent this theory completely by means of a diagram, but the accompanying Figure 6.1 may, perhaps, render it clearer. Suppose the line pqr to be a small portion of the curve of utility of one commodity, while the broken line $p'qr'$ is the like curve of another commodity which has been reversed and superposed on the other. Owing to this reversal, the quantities of the first commodity are measured along the base line from a towards b, whereas those of the second must be measured in the opposite direction. Let units of both commodities be represented by equal lengths: then the little line $a'a$ indicates an increase of the first commodity, and a decrease of the second. Assume the ratio of exchange to be that of unit for unit, or 1 to 1: then, by receiving the commodity $a'a$ the person will gain the utility ad, and lose the utility $a'c$; or he will make a net gain of the utility corresponding to the mixtilinear figure cd. He will, therefore, wish to extend the exchange. If he were to go up to the point b', and were still proceeding, he would, by the next small exchange, receive the utility be, and part with $b'f$; or he would have a net loss of ef: He would, therefore, have gone too far; and it is pretty obvious that the point of intersection, q, defines the place where he would stop with the greatest advantage. It is there that a net gain is converted into a net loss, or rather where, for an infinitely small quantity,

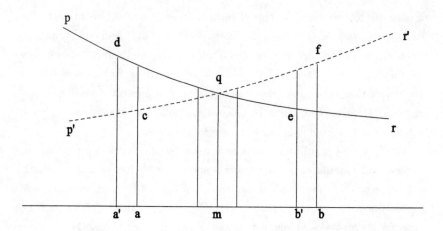

Figure 6.1: Exchange and Utility Curves

there is neither gain nor loss. To represent an infinitely small quantity, or even an exceedingly small quantity, on a diagram is, of course, impossible; but on either side of the line mq I have represented the utilities of a small quantity of commodity more or less, and it is apparent that the net gain or loss upon the exchange of these quantities would be trifling.

Symbolic Statement of the Theory

To represent this process of reasoning in symbols, let Δx denote a small increment of corn, and Δy a small increment of beef exchanged for it. Now our Law of Indifference comes into play. As both the corn and the beef are homogeneous commodities, no parts can be exchanged at a different ratio from other parts in the same market: hence, if x be the whole quantity of corn given for y the whole quantity of beef received, Δy must have the same ratio to Δx as y to x; we have then,

$$\frac{\Delta y}{\Delta x} = \frac{y}{x} \text{ or } \Delta y = \frac{y}{x}\Delta x$$

In a state of equilibrium, the utilities of these increments must be equal in the case of each party, in order that neither more nor less exchange would be desirable. Now the increment of beef, Δy, is $\frac{y}{x}$ times as great as the increment of corn, Δx, so that,

in order that their utilities shall be equal, the degree of utility of beef must be $\frac{x}{y}$ times as great as the degree of utility of corn. Thus we arrive at the principle that *the degrees of utility of commodities exchanged will be in the inverse proportion of the magnitudes of the increments exchanged.*

Let us now suppose that the first body, A, originally possessed the quantity a of corn, and that the second body, B, possessed the quantity b of beef. As the exchange consists in giving x of corn for y of beef, the state of things after exchange will be as follows:

$$A \text{ holds } a - x \text{ of corn, and } y \text{ of beef,}$$
$$B \text{ holds } x \text{ of corn, and } b - y \text{ of beef.}$$

Let $\phi_1 \left(a - x \right)$ denote the final degree of utility of corn to A, and $\phi_2 x$ the corresponding function for B. Also let $\psi_1 y$ denote A's final degree of utility for beef, and $\psi_2 \left(b - y \right)$ B's similar function. Then, ... A will not be satisfied unless the following equation holds true:

$$\phi_1 \left(a - x \right) dx = \psi_1 y dy$$

or

$$\frac{\phi_1 \left(a - x \right)}{\psi_1 y} = \frac{dy}{dx}$$

Hence, substituting for the second member ... we have

$$\frac{\phi_1 \left(a - x \right)}{\psi_1 y} = \frac{y}{x}$$

What holds true of A will also hold true of B, *mutatis mutandis.* He must also derive exactly equal utility from the final increments, otherwise it will be for his interest to exchange either more or less, and he will disturb the conditions of exchange. Accordingly the following equation must hold true:

$$\psi_2 \left(b - y \right) dy = \phi_2 x dx$$

or, substituting as before,

$$\frac{\phi_2 x}{\psi_2 (b - y)} = \frac{y}{x}$$

We arrive, then, at the conclusion, that whenever two commodities are exchanged for each other, and *more or less can be given or received in infinitely small quantities*, the quantities exchanged satisfy two equations, which may be thus stated in a concise form

$$\frac{\phi_1 (a - x)}{\psi_1 y} = \frac{y}{x} = \frac{\phi_2 x}{\psi_2 (b - y)}$$

The two equations are sufficient to determine the results of exchange; for there are only two unknown quantities concerned, namely, x and y, the quantities given and received.

A vague notion has existed in the minds of economical writers, that the conditions of exchange may be expressed in the form of an equation. Thus, J. S. Mill has said: 'The idea of a *ratio*, as between demand and supply, is out of place, and has no concern in the matter: the proper mathematical analogy is that of an *equation*. Demand and supply, the quantity demanded and the quantity supplied, will be made equal.' Mill here speaks of an equation as only a proper mathematical *analogy*. But if Economics is to be a real science at all, it must not deal merely with analogies; it must reason by real equations, like all the other sciences which have reached at all a systematic character. Mill's equation indeed, is not explicitly the same as any at which we have arrived above. His equation states that the quantity of a commodity given by A is equal to the quantity received by B. This seems at first sight to be a mere truism, for this equality must necessarily exist, if any exchange takes place at all. The theory of value, as expounded by Mill, fails to reach the root of the matter, and show how the amount of demand or supply is caused to vary. And Mill does not perceive that, as there must be two parties and two quantities to every exchange, there must be two equations.

Nevertheless, our theory is perfectly consistent with the laws of supply and demand; and if we had the functions of utility determined, it would be possible to throw them into a form clearly expressing the equivalence of supply and demand. We may regard x as the quantity demanded on one side and supplied on the other; similarly, y is the quantity supplied on the one side and demanded on the other. Now, when we hold the two equations to be simultaneously true, we assume that the x and y of one equation equal those of the other. The laws of supply and demand are thus a result of what seems to me the true theory of value or exchange. ...

Complex Cases of the Theory

We have hitherto considered the Theory of Exchange as applying only to two trading bodies possessing and dealing in two commodities. Exactly the same principles hold true, however numerous and complicated may be the conditions. The main point to be remembered in tracing out the results of the theory is, that the same pair of commodities in the same market can have only one ratio of exchange, which must therefore prevail between each body and each other, the costs of conveyance being considered as *nil*. The equations become rapidly more numerous as additional bodies or commodities are considered; but we may exhibit them as they apply to the case of three trading bodies and three commodities.

Thus, suppose that

A possesses the stock a of cotton, and gives
x_1 of it to B, x_2 to C.
B possesses the stock b of silk, and gives
y_1 to A, y_2 to C.
C possesses the stock c of wool, and gives
z_1, to A, z_2 to B.

We have here altogether six unknown quantities – x_1, x_2, y_1, y_2, z_1, z_2; but we have also sufficient means of determining them. They are exchanged as follows

A gives x_1 for y_1, and x_2 for z_1
B gives y_1 for x_1, and y_2 for z_2
C gives z_1 for x_2, and z_2 for y_2

These may be treated as independent exchanges; each body must be satisfied in regard to each of its exchanges, and we must therefore take into account the functions of utility or the final degrees of utility of each commodity in respect of each body. Let us express these functions as follows

ϕ_1, ψ_1, χ_1, are the respective functions of utility for A.

ϕ_2, ψ_2, χ_2, are the respective functions of utility for B.

ϕ_3, ψ_3, χ_3, are the respective functions of utility for C.

Now A, after the exchange, will hold $a - x_1 - x_2$ of cotton and y_1 of silk; and B will hold x_1, of cotton and $b - y_1 - y_2$ of silk: their ratio of exchange, y_1 for x_1 will therefore be governed by the following pair of equations:

$$\frac{\phi_1 (a - x_1 - x_2)}{\psi_1 y_1} = \frac{y_1}{x_1} = \frac{\phi_2 x_1}{\psi_2 (b - y_1 - y_2)}$$

The exchange of A with C will be similarly determined by the ratio of the degrees of utility of wool and cotton on each side subsequent to the exchange; hence we have

$$\frac{\phi_1 (a - x_1 - x_2)}{\chi_1 z_1} = \frac{z_1}{x_2} = \frac{\phi_3 x_2}{\chi_3 (c - z_1 - z_2)}$$

There will also be interchange between B and C which will be independently regulated on similar principles, so that we have another pair of equations to complete the conditions, namely

$$\frac{\psi_2 (b - y_1 - y_2)}{\chi_2 z_2} = \frac{z_2}{y_2} = \frac{\psi_3 y_2}{\chi_3 (c - z_1 - z_2)}$$

We might proceed in the same way to lay down the conditions of exchange between more numerous bodies, but the principles would be exactly the same. For every quantity of commodity which is given in exchange something must be received; and if portions of the same kind of commodity be received from several distinct parties, then we may conceive the quantity which is given for that commodity to be broken up into as many distinct portions. The exchanges in the most complicated case may thus always be decomposed into simple exchanges, and every exchange will give rise to two equations sufficient to determine the quantities involved. The same can also be done when there are two or more commodities in the possession of each trading body.

Competition in Exchange

One case of the Theory of Exchange is of considerable importance, and arises when two parties compete together in supplying a third party with a certain commodity. Thus, suppose that A, with the quantity of one commodity denoted by a, purchases another kind of commodity both from B and from C, who respectively possess b and c of it. All the quantities concerned are as follows

A gives x_1 of a to B and x_2 to C,

B gives y_1 of b to A,

C gives y_2 of c to A.

As each commodity may be supposed to be perfectly homogeneous, the ratio of exchange must be the same in one case as in the other, so that we have one equation thus furnished

$$\frac{y_1}{x_1} = \frac{y_2}{x_2} \tag{6.2}$$

Now, provided that A gets the right commodity in the proper quantity, he does not care whence it comes, so that we need not, in his equation, distinguish the source or destination of the quantities; he simply gives $x_1 + x_2$, and receives in exchange $y_1 + y_2$. Observing, then, that by (6.2)

$$\frac{y_1 + y_2}{x_1 + x_2} = \frac{y_1}{x_1}$$

we have the usual equation of exchange

$$\frac{\phi_1 \left(a - x_1 - x_2\right)}{\psi_1 \left(y_1 + y_2\right)} = \frac{y_1}{x_1} \tag{6.3}$$

But B and C must both be separately satisfied with their shares in the transaction. Thus

$$\frac{\phi_2 x_1}{\psi_2 (b - y_1)} = \frac{y_1}{x_1} \tag{6.4}$$

$$\frac{\phi_3 x_2}{\psi_3 (c - y_2)} = \frac{y_2}{x_2} \tag{6.5}$$

There are altogether four unknown quantities – x_1, x_2, y_1, y_2; and we have four equations by which to determine them. Various suppositions might be made as to the comparative magnitudes of the quantities b and c, or the character of the functions concerned; and conclusions could then be drawn as to the effect upon the trade. The general result would be, that the smaller holder must more or less conform to the prices of the larger holder.

Failure of the Equations of Exchange

Cases constantly occur in which equations of the kind set forth in the preceding pages fail to hold true, or lead to impossible results. Such failure may indicate that no exchange at all takes place, but it may also have a different meaning.

In the first case, it may happen that the commodity possessed by A has a high degree of utility to A, and a low degree to B, and that *vice versa* B's commodity has a high degree of utility to B and less to A. This difference of utility might exist to such an extent, that though B were to receive very little of A's commodity, yet the final degree of utility to him would be less than that of his own commodity, of which he enjoys much more. In such a case no benefit can arise from exchange, and no exchange will consequently take place. This failure of exchange will be indicated by a failure of the equations.

It may also happen that the whole quantities of commodity possessed are exchanged, and yet the equations fail. A may have so low a desire for consuming his own commodity, that the very last increment of it has less degree of utility to him than a small addition to the commodity received in exchange. The same state of things might happen to exist with B as regards his commodity: under these circumstances the whole possessions of one might be exchanged for the whole of the other, and the ratio of exchange would of course be defined by the ratio of these quantities. Yet each party might desire the last increment of the commodity received more than he desires the last increment of that given, so that the equations would fail to be true. ...

The Gain by Exchange

It is a most important result of this theory that the ratio of exchange gives no indication of the real benefit derived from the action of exchange. So many trades are occupied in buying and selling, and make their profits by buying low and selling high, that there arises a fallacious tendency to believe that the whole benefit of trade depends upon the differences of prices. It is implied that to pay a high price is worse than doing without the article, and the whole financial system of a great nation may be distorted in the effort to carry out a false theory.

This is the result to which some of J.S. Mill's remarks, in his *Theory of International Trade*, would lead. That theory is always ingenious, and as it seems to me, nearly always true; but he draws from it the following conclusion: 'The countries which carry on their foreign trade on the most advantageous terms are those whose commodities are most in demand by foreign countries, and which have themselves the least demand for foreign commodities. From which, among other consequences, it follows that the richest countries, *ceteris paribus*, gain the least by a given amount of foreign commerce: since, having a greater demand for commodities generally, they are likely to have a greater demand for foreign commodities, and thus modify the terms of interchange to their own disadvantage. Their aggregate gains by foreign trade, doubtless, are generally greater than those of poorer countries, since they carry on a greater amount of such trade, and gain the benefit of cheapness on a larger consumption: but their gain is less on each individual article consumed.'

In the absence of any explanation to the contrary, this passage must be taken to mean that the advantage of foreign trade depends upon the terms of exchange, and that international trade is less advantageous to a rich than to a poor country. But such a conclusion involves confusion between two distinct things – the price of a commodity and its total utility. A country is not merely like a great mercantile firm buying and selling goods, and making a profit out of the difference of price; it buys goods in order to consume them. But, in estimating the benefit which a consumer derives from a commodity, it is the total utility which must be taken as the measure, not the final degree of utility on which the terms of exchange depend. ...

So far is Mill's statement from being fundamentally correct, that I believe the truth lies in the opposite direction. As a general rule, the greatness of the price which a country is willing and able to pay for the productions of other countries, measures, or at least manifests, the greatness of the benefit which it derives from such imports. He who pays a high price must either have a very great need of that which he buys, or very little need of that which he pays for it; on either supposition there is gain by exchange. In questions of this sort there is but one rule which can be safely laid down, namely, that no one will buy a thing unless he expects advantage from the purchase; and perfect freedom of exchange, therefore, tends to the maximising of utility.

One advantage of the Theory of Economics, carefully studied, will be to make us very careful in our conclusions when the matter is not of the simplest possible nature. The fact that we can most imperfectly estimate the total utility of any one commodity should prevent us, for instance, from attempting to measure the benefit of any trade.

6.5 Walras

This section contains selected material from Lessons 5 and 6 of Walras (1954, pp.86-126), first published in 1874. Here he provides a non-utility extension of the ealier model of Cournot (see chapter 5 above) and then explains how, in principle, demand curves can be derived from utility maximisation.

Elements of Pure Economics

Problem of Exchange of Two Commodities

We shall study value in exchange as it arises under such competitive conditions ... We may take any two commodities, say oats and wheat, or, more abstractly, (A) and (B). I put the letters A and B in parentheses whenever I wish to indicate that these letters do not represent *quantities*, which are the only things that can be used in equations, but rather kinds or species or, as one might say in philosophical terms, *essences*.

Let us now imagine a market to which some people come holding commodity (A), ready to exchange part of it in order to procure commodity (B); while others come holding commodity (B), ready to exchange part of their (B) in order to procure commodity (A). Since the bidding will have to start at some point or other, we shall suppose that a broker offers to give up n units of (B) for m units of (A) in accordance, let us say, with the closing rate of exchange of the preceding day. This bid will conform to the equation of exchange

$$mv_a = nv_b$$

in which v_a is the value in exchange of one unit of (A) and v_b is the value in exchange of one unit of (B).

Let us define prices in general as ratios between values in exchange or as relative values in exchange. In general, also, let us designate the price of (B) in terms of (A) by p_b, and the price of (A) in terms of (B) by p_a. If, then, we

denote, in the particular case we are dealing with, the quotients of the ratios
$\frac{m}{n}$ and $\frac{n}{m}$ by μ and $\frac{1}{\mu}$ respectively, it follows from the above equation that

$$\frac{v_b}{v_a} = p_b = \frac{m}{n} = \mu$$

$$\frac{v_a}{v_b} = p_a = \frac{n}{m} = \frac{1}{\mu}$$

and from these two that

$$p_b = \frac{1}{p_a}, \qquad p_a = \frac{1}{p_b}$$

Thus: *Prices, or ratios of values in exchange, are equal to the inverse ratios of the quantities exchanged.*

The price of any one commodity in terms of another is the reciprocal of the price of the second commodity in terms of the first.

If (A) were oats and (B) wheat, and a broker had offered to exchange 5 hectolitres of wheat for 10 hectolitres of oats, then the bid price of wheat in terms of oats would be 2, and that of oats in terms of wheat would be 1/2. We have already observed that there is always a double sale and a double purchase in every exchange transaction; correspondingly there is also a double price. It is of the utmost importance that the invariable reciprocal nature of the relationship between the two prices in any exchange be fully understood, and the use of algebraic symbols is particularly useful in this connection because it makes this reciprocal relationship stand out in the clearest possible relief. Furthermore, it is seen that these symbols have the advantage of being conducive to a clear and precise formulation of general propositions. That is why we shall continue to use them.

Let D_a, O_a, D_b and O_b be the effective demand and offer of commodities (A) and (B) at their respective prices $p_a = \frac{1}{\mu}$ and $p_b = \mu$. Between the quantities demanded, quantities offered and prices there is a fundamental relationship, which we must examine before we do anything else.

Effective demand and effective offer are, as we have seen, the demand and the offer of a given quantity of a commodity at a given price. Consequently,

to say that a quantity D_a of (A) is demanded at the price p_a is, *ipso facto*
the same thing as saying that a quantity O_b of (B), equal to $D_a p_a$, is being
offered. For example, to say that there is a demand for 200 hectolitres of
oats at the price 1/2 in terms of wheat is, by virtue of that fact alone, the
same as saying that 100 hectolitres of wheat are being offered. It follows that
in general the relationship between D_a, p_a and O_b can be expressed by the
equation

$$O_b = D_a p_a$$

In like manner, to say that a quantity O_a of (A) is offered at the price
p_a, is, *ipso facto* the same thing as saying that a quantity D_b of (B), equal
to $O_a p_a$, is being demanded. For example, to say that 150 hectolitres of oats
are being offered at the price of 1/2 in terms of wheat is, by virtue of that
fact alone, the same as saying that there is a demand for 75 hectolitres of
wheat. It follows that in general the relations between O_a, p_a and D_b can
always be expressed by the equation

$$D_b = O_a p_a$$

It could be proved, in like manner, that D_b, O_b, p_b, O_a and D_a are related
according to the following equations:

$$O_a = D_b p_b$$

$$D_a = O_b p_b \qquad .$$

but it would be superfluous to do so, since these last two equations follow
from the two previous ones together with the equation

$$P_a P_b = 1$$

Thus: *The effective demand for or offer of one commodity in exchange
for another is equal respectively to the effective offer of or demand for the
second commodity multiplied by its price in terms of the first.*

Evidently, any two of the four quantities, D_a, O_a, D_b and O_b, will determine the other two. For the present we shall assume that the quantities offered, O_a and O_b, are determined by the quantities demanded, D_a and D_b respectively, and not the other way round. Indeed, demand ought to be considered as the principal fact and offer as the accessory fact where two commodities are exchanged for each other in kind. No one ever makes an offer simply for the sake of offering. The only reason one offers anything is that one cannot demand anything without making an offer. Offer is only a consequence of demand. Consequently, to begin with, we shall confine ourselves to the indirect relationship between offer and price, and study direct relationships only in so far as they subsist between demand and price. At prices p_a and p_b, D_a and D_b are demanded, whence we deduce that $O_a = D_b p_b$ and $O_b = D_a p_a$ are being offered.

This being so, if we let

$$D_a = \alpha O_a$$

then we may make any one of three suppositions, according as $\alpha = 1$, $\alpha > 1$ or $\alpha < 1$. But, before going into that, let us state a final theorem.

If in the above equation we substitute for D_a and O_a the values given by the equations

$$D_a = O_b p_b$$

and

$$O_a = D_b p_b$$

we obtain

$$O_b = \alpha D_b$$

Thus: *Given two commodities the ratio of the effective demand of either one of them to its effective offer is equal to the ratio of the effective offer of the other to its effective demand.*

This theorem may be deduced as follows:

$$D_a = O_b p_b$$

$$D_b = O_a p_a$$

$$D_a D_b = O_a O_b$$

or, in like manner:

$$
\begin{aligned}
O_a &= D_b p_b \\
O_b &= D_a p_a \\
O_a O_b &= D_a D_b
\end{aligned}
$$

In either case it follows that

$$\frac{O_b}{D_b} = \frac{D_a}{O_a} = \alpha$$

It is to be observed that if the effective demand for and effective offer of (A) are equal, the effective offer of and effective demand for (B) will also be equal. We see, too, that if the effective demand for (A) is greater than its effective offer, then the effective offer of (B) will be proportionately greater than its effective demand. Finally, if the effective offer of (A) is greater than its effective demand, then the effective demand for (B) will be proportionately greater than its effective offer. This is the meaning of the above theorem.

Now suppose that $\alpha = 1$, $D_a = O_a$ and $O_b = D_b$; that the quantities demanded and quantities offered of each of the two commodities (A) and (B) are equal at their respective prices, $p_a = \frac{1}{\mu}$ and $p_b = \mu$; and that each buyer and each seller finds a corresponding seller and a corresponding buyer with the exact counterpart of his bid or offer. The market will be in equilibrium. At the equilibrium prices $\frac{1}{\mu}$ and μ, the quantity $D_a = O_a$ of (A) will be exchanged for the quantity $O_b = D_b$ of (B), and at the close of the market, each party to the exchange will go his own way.

... How then can equality between the demand for and the offer of each of the two commodities be reached?

The first idea that comes to mind is to repeat purely and simply the line of reasoning which we developed earlier in our discussion of Rentes in the stock exchange. But that would be an egregious error. What we had in our example drawn from the stock exchange were buyers and sellers of Rentes, that is, of securities the value of which depended both on the particular yield of these securities and on the general rate of return on capital. As we shall see later, the only possible result that could follow from a rise in the price of

Rentes would be a decrease in the demand for them and an increase in their offer; and the only possible result that could follow from a fall in their price would be an increase in the demand for them and decrease in their offer. In our present example, traders exchange nothing but (A) and (B), which are assumed to possess direct utility and to be the only commodities which can be exchanged for each other in the market. This circumstance alters everything.

To be sure, it will still be necessary to raise p_a (or lower p_b), whenever D_a is greater than O_a, or, contrariwise, to raise p_b (or lower p_a) whenever D_b is greater than O_b. Moreover, there is no doubt that our previous reasoning about demand still holds good. As the price increases, demand cannot increase; it can only decrease. Moreover, as price decreases, demand cannot decrease; it can only increase. Let us imagine a trader holding 12 hectolitres of wheat who offers 5 of them for 10 hectolitres of oats, or, in other words, who demands 10 hectolitres of oats at the price 0.50 in terms of wheat. At this price 0.50 of oats, in terms of wheat, he could have bought as many as 24 hectolitres of oats, but his own need for wheat compels him to restrict his demand for oats to 10 hectolitres. At the price 0.60, he could purchase at most 20 hectolitres of oats; and it must be admitted that, in view of his own wheat requirements, he would have to content himself with an amount of oats at most equal to, but more likely less than, the 10 hectolitres which he had been able to get when he was better off. Thus a rise in p_a, which is the same thing as a fall in p_b, can only decrease D_a and increase D_b. *Per contra*, a rise in p_b, which is the same thing as a fall in p_a, can only decrease D_b and increase D_a. But what will happen to O_a and O_b? It is impossible to tell. O_a is equal to the product of D_b multiplied by p_b. Now, if either one of the two factors, say p_b, decreases or increases, the other factor must increase or decrease in consequence. Likewise O_b is equal to the product of D_a multiplied by p_a. As p_a increases or decreases, D_a must decrease or increase in consequence. How can we tell, then, whether we are approaching equilibrium?

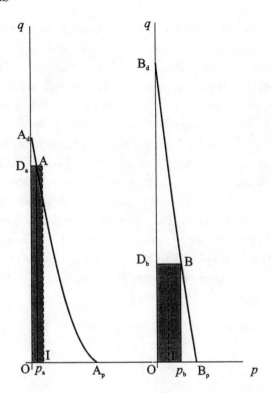

Figure 6.2: Effective Offer and Demand

Effective Offer and Demand

... Geometrically the problem consists in inscribing within the two curves A_dA_p and B_dB_p of Figure 6.2 two rectangles, OD_aAp_a and OD_bBp_b, respectively, such that their bases are reciprocals of each other, while their altitudes are so related that the altitude of the first OD_a is equal to the area of the second $OD_b \times Op_b$ and, conversely, the altitude of the second OD_b is equal to the area of the first $OD_a \times Op_a$. The bases of these two rectangles, Op_a and Op_b, represent equilibrium prices, in as much as at these prices the demand for (A), represented by the altitude OD_a equals the offer of (A) represented by the area $OD_b \times Op_b$, and the demand for (B) represented by the altitude OD_b equals the offer of (B) represented by the area $OD_a \times Op_a$.

In saying that *the altitude of either rectangle is equal to the area of the other*, I have been equating terms that are not homogeneous. But under the circumstances homogeneity is not necessary, since the condition that the bases be reciprocals of each other implies the predetermination of a common unit, say OI, which was used in the construction of both curves. To make the point still clearer, I might add that the height of each rectangle should contain as many of these predetermined units of length as the other rectangle contains similar units of area; or, alternatively, that this area of each rectangle should equal the area of a rectangle having the same altitude as the other rectangle but with a base one unit in length. It follows, moreover, from the terms of the problem that the base of either rectangle is equal to the inverse ratio of the altitude of that rectangle to the altitude of the other and to the direct ratio of the area of that rectangle to the area of the other.

Algebraically the problem consists in finding the two roots, p_a and p_b of one of the following pairs of equations:

$$F_a\left(p_a\right) = F_b\left(p_b\right)p_b$$
$$p_a p_b = 1$$

or

$$F_a\left(p_a\right)p_a = F_b\left(p_b\right)$$
$$p_a p_b = 1$$

or, alternatively, of two equations which are expressions of equality between D_a, and O_a, and between D_b, and O_b respectively:

$$F_a\left(p_a\right) = F_b\left(\frac{1}{p_a}\right)\frac{1}{p_a}$$
$$F_a\left(\frac{1}{p_b}\right)\frac{1}{p_b} = F_b\left(p_b\right)$$

Moreover, the geometric and algebraic methods may be combined into one. Starting with the known curves $A_d A_p$ and $B_d B_p$, or their equations

$$D_a = F_a\left(p_a\right)$$

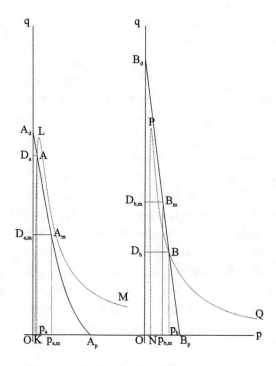

Figure 6.3: Demand and Supply Curves

and

$$D_b = F_b\left(p_b\right)$$

respectively, let us now draw the curves KLM and NPQ (Figure 6.3) with the equations

$$O_a = F_b\left(\frac{1}{p_b}\right)\frac{1}{p_a}$$

and

$$O_b = F_a\left(\frac{1}{p_b}\right)\frac{1}{p_b}$$

KLM will intersect A_dA_p at the point A, and NPQ will intersect B_dB_p at the point B, i.e. at those very points which give us the rectangles we have described above.

It is easy to interpret the meaning of the dotted curves, KLM and NPQ, and to see how they are drawn.

The first curve KLM is an offer curve of (A), no longer identified with the demand curve of (B) which represented the offer of (A) as a function of p_b by means of the areas of inscribed rectangles constructed on the co-ordinate axes, but distinct, depicting this same offer of (A) by the ordinates as a function of p_a.

The curve starts from zero for an infinitely high price of (A) in terms of (B), corresponding to an infinitesimally small price of (B) in terms of (A). In other words, KLM is asymptotic to the price axis. The curve rises as we move along it towards the origin, with each fall in the price of (A) in terms of (B) corresponding to a rise in the price of (B) in terms of (A). It reaches its maximum [ordinate] at the point L the abscissa of which represents a price of (A) in terms of (B) such that its reciprocal $p_{b,m}$, i.e. the price of (B) in terms of (A) measured by the abscissa $Op_{b,m}$, of the point B_m is the price at which the rectangle inscribed within $B_d B_p$ is a maximum. Then the curve KLM falls as we move along it towards the origin until its ordinate becomes zero again at a price of (A) in terms of (B) represented by the length OK, this price being the reciprocal of the price of (B) in terms of (A) measured by the abscissa OB_p of the point B_p where the curve $B_d B_p$ meets the price axis.

Similarly, the second curve NPQ is an offer curve of (B), no longer identified with the demand curve of (A) which represented the offer of (B) as a function of p_a by means of the areas of inscribed rectangles constructed on the co-ordinate axes, but distinct, depicting this same offer of (B) by the ordinates as a function of p_b.

This curve starts from zero for an infinitely high price of (B) in terms of (A), corresponding to an infinitesimally small price of (A) in terms of (B). In other words, NPQ is asymptotic to the price axis. The curve rises as we move along it towards the origin, with each fall in the price of (B) in terms of (A) corresponding to a rise in the price of (A) in terms of (B). It reaches its maximum at the point P, the abscissa of which represents a price of (B) in terms of (A) such that its reciprocal $p_{a,m}$, i.e. the price of (A) in terms of (B) measured by the abscissa $Op_{a,m}$ of the point A_m is the price at which the rectangle inscribed within A_dA_p is a maximum. Then the curve NPQ falls as we move along it towards the origin until its ordinate becomes zero again at a price of (B) in terms of (A) represented by the length ON, this price being the reciprocal of the price of (A) in terms of (B) measured by the abscissa OA_p of the point A_p where the curve A_dA_p meets the price axis.

It is obvious that the shapes of the curves KLM and NPQ are intimately related to the shapes of B_dB_p and A_dA_p respectively. If we had supposed the latter curves to be different, the former, too, would have been entirely different. At all events, in the diagram we have just been discussing, the curve B_dB_p passes, while falling from left to right, through the point B_m *before* cutting the dotted curve NPQ at a point where NPQ is rising as we move along it *from its zero ordinate to its maximum ordinate at P*; and, consequently, the curve A_dA_p passes, while it too falls from left to right, through the point A_m after cutting the dotted curve KLM at a point where KLM is falling as we move along it *from its maximum ordinate L to its zero ordinate.*

Now, under these circumstances, it is evident that if the two curves A_dA_p and KLM intersect at the point A, then the curve A_dA_p lies *below* the curve KLM *to the right* of this point and *above* the curve KLM to the left; and it is likewise evident that if the two curves B_dB_p and NPQ intersect at the point B, then the curve B_dB_p lies *below* the curve NPQ to the right of this point and above the curve NPQ *to the left.*

Thus, since $p_a = \frac{1}{\mu}$ and $p_b = \mu$ are, by hypothesis, the prices at which $D_a = O_a$ and $O_b = D_b$ it follows that at all prices of (A) in terms of (B) higher than p_a, corresponding to prices of (B) in terms of (A) lower than p_b, $O_a > D_a$ and $D_b > O_b$. Conversely, at all prices of (A) in terms of (B) lower than p_a corresponding to prices of (B) in terms of (A) higher than p_b, $D_a > O_a$ and $O_b > D_b$. In the first case, the equilibrium price could only be restored by an increase in p_b corresponding to a decrease in p_a; whereas in the second case equilibrium price could only be restored by an increase in p_a corresponding to a decrease in p_b.

We are now ready to formulate in the following terms *the law of effective offer and effective demand or the law of the establishment of equilibrium* *prices* in the case of the exchange of two commodities for each other: *Given* *two commodities, for the market to be in equilibrium with respect to these* *commodities, or for the price of either commodity to be stationary in terms* *of the other, it is necessary and sufficient that the effective demand be equal* *to the effective offer of each commodity. Where this equality does not obtain,* *in order to reach equilibrium price, the commodity having an effective demand* *greater than its effective offer must rise in price, and the commodity having* *an effective offer greater than its effective demand must fall in price.*

... We are now in a position to see clearly what the mechanism of market competition is. It is the practical solution, reached through a rise or fall in prices, of the same problem of exchange to which we have just given a theoretical and mathematical solution; but it must be understood that we do not have the slightest idea of substituting one solution for the other. The rapidity and reliability of the practical solution leave no room for improvement. It is a matter of daily experience that even in big markets where there are neither brokers nor auctioneers, the current equilibrium price is determined within a few minutes, and considerable quantities of merchandise are exchanged at that price within half or three quarters of an hour. In fact, the theoretical solution would be absolutely impracticable in almost every case. On the other hand, it is no valid objection against our method to speak of the difficulty of deriving curves or equations of exchange. Whether there is any advantage to be found in constructing all or part of either the demand or the offer curve of a given commodity in certain cases, and whether it is possible or impossible to do so, are questions on which we reserve judgement entirely. For the moment, we are examining the problem of exchange in general, and the conception, pure and simple, of curves of exchange is sufficient and at the same time indispensable. ...

The Theorem of Maximum Utility

... let the term *effective utility* designate the sum total of wants satisfied by any given *quantity consumed* of a commodity ...

Analytically, if we are given effective utilities as functions of the quantities consumed according to the equations $u = \Phi_{a,1}(q)$ and $u = \Phi_{b,1}(q)$, then the *raretés* are designated by the derivatives, $\Phi'_{a,1}(q)$ and $\Phi'_{b,1}(q)$. If, on the other hand, we are given the *raretés* as functions of the quantities consumed, according to the equations $r = \phi_{a,1}(q)$ and $r = \phi_{b,1}(q)$ then the effective utilities are designated by the definite integrals from 0 to q : $\int_0^q \phi_{a,1}(q)dq$ and $\int_0^q \phi_{b,1}(q)dq$. We then have for u and r the mutually related expressions

$$u = \Phi(q) = \int_0^q \phi(q)\, dq$$

and

$$r = \Phi'(q) = \phi(q)$$

... The problem which was to be solved may now be stated as follows: *Given two commodities (A) and (B), given each party's utility or want curves for these commodities, and given the initial stock which each party possesses, to determine the demand curves.*

We shall do well to reformulate this solution in the customary notation of the infinitesimal calculus.

Let d_a be the quantity of (A) which will be demanded, and $o_b = d_a p_a$ be the quantity of (B) which will be offered at the price p_a of (A) in terms of (B); and, consequently, let $q_b - o_b$ be the quantity of (B) which will be retained, so that we have

$$d_a p_a + (q_b - o_b) = q_b \tag{6.6}$$

where q_b is the initial stock of (B) possessed by a given holder.

Moreover, let $u = \Phi_{a,1}(q)$ and $u = \Phi_{b,1}(q)$ be the two equations denoting the effective utilities of (A) and (B) respectively for our individual as functions of the quantities consumed; and let

$$\Phi_{a,1}(d_a) + \Phi_{b,1}(q_b - o_b)$$

be, therefore, the total effective utility to be maximized. Since the derivatives of the Φ functions are essentially decreasing, the maximum which our party to the exchange seeks will be found when the algebraic sum of the differential increments of utility with respect to the quantities consumed of each of the two commodities is zero. For, if we suppose these increments to be unequal and opposite in sign, our party will find it to his advantage to demand more or less of the commodity of which the differential increment is larger or smaller and to offer in return more or less of the commodity of which the differential increment is smaller or larger. The condition of maximum satisfaction of wants can now be expressed by the equation

$$\Phi'_{a,1}\left(d_a\right) dd_a + \Phi'_{b,1}\left(q_b - o_b\right) d\left(q_b - o_b\right) = 0$$

Now, on the one hand, the derivatives of the functions of effective utility with respect to the quantities consumed are none other than the *raretés*; while, on the other hand, the algebraic sum of the products of the prices of the two commodities in terms of one of them multiplied by the differentials of the quantities consumed is, by virtue of equation (6.6), equal to zero according to the equation

$$p_a dd_a + d\left(q_b - o_b\right) = 0$$

It follows from this that

$$\phi_{a,1}\left(d_a\right) = p_a \phi_{b,1}\left(q_b - d_a p_a\right)$$

... by differentiating either of the following two expressions with respect to d_a:

$$\Phi_{a,1}\left(d_a\right) + \Phi_{b,1}\left(q_b - d_a p_a\right)$$

or

$$\int_o^{d_a} \phi_{a,1}\left(q\right) dq + \int_o^{q_b - d_a p_a} \phi_{b,1}\left(q\right) dq$$

we obtain

$$\phi_{a,1}\left(d_a\right) - p_a \phi_{b,1}\left(q_b - d_a p_a\right) = 0$$

or

$$\phi_{a,1}\left(d_a\right) = p_a \phi_{b,1}\left(q_b - d_a p_a\right)$$

It will be readily seen also that the root of this derived equation always corresponds to a maximum and not a minimum, because the functions $\Phi'_{a,1}(q)$ or, $\phi_{a,1}(q)$ and $\Phi'_{b,1}(q)$ or $\phi_{b,1}(q)$ are by their nature decreasing and the second derivative

$$\phi'_{a,1}(d_a) + p_a^2 \phi'_{b,1}(q_b - d_a p_a)$$

is necessarily negative.

Chapter 7

Marshall and Edgeworth

7.1 Marshall

This section contains material from Marshall (1975, pp.129-157), first privately circulated in 1879. Here he presents his extension of Mill's international trade analysis, involving reciprocal demand or offer curves. It is followed by Marshall's note XII to his appendix on barter from his Principles (1961, pp.844-845), in which he examines Edgeworth's barter model with trading at disequilibrium prices.

The Pure Theory of Foreign Trade

The Premises of the Pure Theory of Foreign trade. The Method of Diagrams. The Fundamental Laws of curves which Represent International Demand

The function of a pure theory is to deduce definite conclusions from definite hypothetical premises. The premises should approximate as closely as possible to the facts with which the corresponding applied theory has to deal. But the terms used in the pure theory must be capable of exact interpretation, and the hypotheses on which it is based must be simple and easily handled.

The pure theory of foreign trade satisfies these conditions. This theory is based upon the hypothesis that two countries, say England and Germany, carry on trade with each other but only with each other. It is assumed that they are not under any obligations to make foreign payments excepting those arising from trade, so that in equilibrium the exports of each country exchange for her imports. It is assumed that the pure theory of domestic values has provided the means of measuring the value in England of all the various wares exported by England in terms of any one of them. Suppose cloth of a definite quality to be one of them; then the value, in England, of all the wares which England exports may be expressed as that of a certain number of yards of cloth. So the value in Germany of all the wares which Germany exports, may be expressed as that of, say, a certain number of yards of linen.

We may for brevity use the phrase 'a certain number of yards of cloth,' as a substitute for the complete phrase 'English wares the equivalent of a certain number of yards of cloth': and so for linen. Further we may consider that the processes of producing the cloth and the linen are not completed until the cloth and the linen are delivered in Germany and England respectively. By this means we shall avoid the necessity of specially mentioning the expenses of transport; so that we shall find no occasion to follow Mill in making the assumption that the expenses of transport may be neglected.

We may apply this method of speaking to express the conditions under which trade is in equilibrium; i.e. is such that there is no tendency for the imports and exports of the countries in question to increase or to diminish. Thus: In equilibrium a certain number, say ten million, of yards of cloth are exported annually to Germany and sold there for a price which covers the expenses of producing a certain number, say fifteen million, of yards of linen. Vice versa, fifteen million yards of linen are exported to England and sold there for a price which covers the expense of producing ten million yards of cloth.

We are now in a position to give a definite interpretation to the phrase 'the rate of interchange between two countries' in place of the inexact account sometimes given. We may measure the rate of interchange between England and Germany by the amount of linen which England obtains in return for each yard of cloth which she exports.

It seems on the whole best thus to represent the value of the wares which England exports as equivalent to that of a certain number of yards of cloth. But we might measure it as equivalent to a certain number of units of English capital and labour, or as we may say as equivalent to a certain number of units of English cost of production. We should then measure the rate of interchange between England and Germany by the number of units of German cost of production which England obtains in return for the produce of a given number of units of her cost of production. This latter method of measurement has several advantages, and there is no reason why it should not be adopted in the treatment of some portions of the pure theory of foreign trade. But for the general purposes of the theory the method of measurement first given will be found to be the most convenient.

The theory of foreign trade is necessarily difficult. Mill when introducing it says, 'I must give notice that we are now in the region of the most complicated questions which Political Economy affords; that the subject is one which cannot possibly be made elementary; and that a more continuous effort of attention than has been required, will be necessary to follow the series of deductions'. The unavoidable difficulties of the subject are great: but students frequently fall into errors which they may easily avoid if they will resolve that when discussing the pure theory they will not speak of the imports or exports of a country as measured in terms of money. . . .

The pure theory of economic science requires the aid of an apparatus which can grasp and handle the general quantitative relations on the assumption of which the theory is based. The most powerful engines for such a purpose are supplied by the various branches of mathematical calculus. But diagrams are of great service, wherever they are applicable, in interpreting to the eye the processes by which the methods of mathematical analysis obtain their results. It happens that with a few unimportant exceptions all the results which have been obtained by the application of mathematical methods to pure economic theory can be obtained independently by the method of diagrams.

Diagrams present simultaneously to the eye the chief forces which are at work, laid out, as it were in a map; and thereby suggest results to which attention has not been directed by the use of the methods of mathematical analysis. The method of diagrams can be freely used by every one who is capable of exact reasoning, even though he have no knowledge of Mathematics.

The reader, who will take the trouble to assure himself that he thoroughly understands the account of the curves given in the following paragraphs, will not find difficulty in following the reasoning to which they are afterwards applied. ...

Let us now commence to interpret the laws of international demand into the language of diagrams. Let distances measured along a fixed straight line Ox (Figure 7.1) represent numbers of yards of cloth. Let distances measured along a straight line Oy at right angles to Ox represent numbers of yards of linen. Let a curve OE be drawn as follows: N being any point upon Oy, let it be determined from a knowledge of the circumstances of England's demand for linen, what is the number of yards of cloth, the expenses of producing and exporting which will be covered annually by the proceeds of the sale in England of an amount of linen represented by ON. From Ox measure off OM, equal to this number of yards of cloth. Draw lines through M and N at right angles to Ox and Oy respectively, meeting in P; then P is a point on the required curve, OE. If N be moved from O gradually along Oy, P will assume a series of positions, each of which corresponds to one position of N; the continuous string of points thus formed will be the curve OE. (In other words, OE will be the locus of P.) If we were applying the method of diagrams to the trade that is actually carried on between two countries, we could not indeed obtain trustworthy data for drawing more than a limited portion of the curve. For it is not possible to conjecture with any approach to certainty what would be the terms on which it would be possible to sell in a country an amount of imports, either very much greater, or very much less, than that which is actually sold there. But for the purposes of the pure theory we are at liberty to suppose that the curve is properly drawn throughout its entire length. We may call OE 'England's demand curve'; and bearing in mind that PM is equal to ON, we may describe it thus:

England's demand curve is such that any point P being taken on it, and PM being drawn perpendicular to Ox; OM represents the amount of cloth which England will be willing to give annually for an amount of linen represented by PM.

In exactly the same way we may construct a curve OG which may be

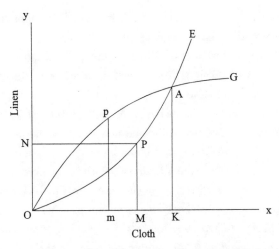

Figure 7.1: Offer Curves for Linen and Cloth

called Germany's demand curve, and which may be described thus:

Germany's demand curve is such that any point p being taken upon it and pm being drawn perpendicular to Ox; pm represents the amount of linen which Germany will be willing to give annually for an amount of cloth represented by Om.

It may not be superfluous to state explicitly that the period for which the supplies of cloth and linen are reckoned is taken as a year only for the purposes of definiteness and brevity. If the phrase 'in a given unit of time' were not cumbrous, it might be substituted throughout for the word 'annually'.

The terms in which the curves are described imply that there is no change in the circumstances which govern the amount or linen that England is willing to take at each particular rate of interchange: and similarly that the circumstances which govern the German demand for cloth remain constant. As a matter of fact the causes which govern the demand of a country for foreign wares do vary from time to time. They are altered by every change that affects her power of raising on the one hand the wares which she exports, and on the other domestic rivals to the wares which she imports; by almost every invention, and almost every change of fashion. But, as has been already said, we should aim at simplicity in our first approximations, in order that they may be easily manageable. Therefore, we are to neglect for the present all consideration of the disturbances arising from such variations; leaving account to be taken of them in the applications of the results of the pure theory to practical issues.

We may now interpret into the language of curves the laws of international demand. The first proposition to be laid down requires no proof. It is that corresponding to every statement that can be made with regard to the terms on which England may be willing to export cloth in exchange for linen there is a similar statement with regard to the terms on which Germany may be willing to export linen in exchange for cloth. Or in other words:

PROP I. *Every statement as to the shape which it is possible for OE to assume, has corresponding to it a similar statement as to the shape which it is possible for OG to assume; but wherever Ox occurs in the former statement, Oy will occur in the latter, and vice versa; whenever reference is made to a horizontal straight line in the former, there must be made reference in the latter to a vertical straight line, and vice versa. ...*

Stable and Unstable Equilibrium of Foreign Trade

It will be convenient to have a name for the point which corresponds to the actual position of the trade between England and Germany at any time. It generally happens in fact that the exports and imports of a country are not distributed evenly all over the year. Allowance must be made for these irregularities before the results of the pure theory can be applied to practice. But for the purposes of the pure theory it is allowable to assume that the importation and the consumption of foreign wares is distributed evenly all over the year.

Thus we may say that cloth is at any time being imported into Germany on the scale of OM annually (or in a given unit of time); meaning thereby that the scale on which it is being imported is such that if it were to continue, the amount imported in the year (or unit of time) would be OM.

We have then the following:

DEFINITION. If at any time cloth be exported from England on the scale of OM annually, in exchange for linen on the scale of ON annually; and MP, NP be drawn at right angles to Ox, Oy respectively, meeting in P; then P is the exchange index at that time.

It has been proved ... that the trade is in equilibrium when the exchange-index is at any point of intersection of OE and OG. In the present chapter it will be shown that some points of intersection correspond to stable equilibrium of the trade and others to unstable: and a fundamental law will be laid down by which the one set may be distinguished from the other. It will be convenient to commence by supposing that the exchange-index is not at A: but that some external disturbing force, as a war, or a bad harvest, has jerked the exchange-index to some position such that the trade corresponding to it is not in equilibrium; and to investigate the forces which will govern its motion.

We know ... that OE cannot cut a horizontal straight line through P more than once: and that OG cannot cut a vertical straight line through P more than once. We may have therefore the following:

DEFINITION. A point P is said to be *to the right* or *to the left* of OE according as it is to the right or the left of the point in which OE is cut by the horizontal straight line through P: and the point P is said to be above or below OG according as it is *above* or *below* the point in which OG is cut by a vertical straight line through P.

The greater part of the pure theory of foreign trade consists of a series of corollaries from the laws with regard to the shapes of OE and OG, which were laid down in the last chapter, together with the following law:

PROP XI. *If the Exchange-index be at any time to the right of OE it will tend to move to the left; if it be to the left of OE it will tend to move to the right. Similarly, if the exchange-index be at any time above OG it will tend to move down-wards; if it be below OG it will tend to move upwards.*

Such interpretation as this proposition may require will be contained in the proof of it. It must be remembered it is assumed throughout that the export trade of each country is conducted by private traders competing against one another. So that when the terms on which a country's foreign trade is conducted are such as to afford a rate of profits higher than the rate current

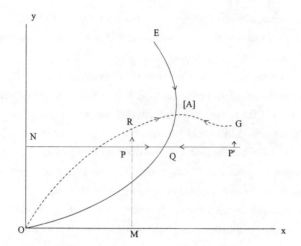

Figure 7.2: Stability of Equilibrium

in other industries, the competition of traders to obtain these higher profits will lead to an increase in the exportation of her wares: and *vice versa* when the rate of profits in the foreign trade is exceptionally low.

Let the exchange-point P be to the left of OE, as in Figure 7.2 and let NP produced cut OE in Q. Then since Q is a point on OE, ON linen is capable or being disposed of annually in England in exchange for the means of producing and exporting NQ cloth. But at the time in question linen is being imported on the scale of ON annually, and cloth is being exported in exchange for it on the scale of only NP annually. Consequently the exportation of cloth in exchange for linen must be a trade which affords abnormally high profits. Consequently, since competition in the trade is supposed to be free, the exportation of cloth will increase. Therefore when the exchange index is to the left of OE it will tend to move to the right. So if the exchange-point lay at P' in NQ produced, it would show that cloth was being exported at the rate of NP' annually in exchange for an amount of linen ON, which could be disposed of in England only for the expenses of producing and exporting NQ cloth: consequently the exportation of cloth would tend to diminish, i.e. when the exchange-point is to the right of OE, it will tend to move to the left.

Similar proofs apply to the second part of the proposition which relates to OG.

In order therefore to determine the directions in which the amounts of the exports of cloth and linen are tending to change at any time, it is requisite only to determine the position of the exchange-index at that time and through it to draw arrowheads – an arrowhead pointing towards the right if the exchange-index lies on the left of OE, towards the left if this point lies on the right of OE, and an arrowhead pointing upwards if the exchange-index lies below OG, downwards if this point lies above OG.[1]

The exchange-index will in each case tend to move in some direction within the angle made by the arrowheads. Thus, if the exchange-index be at P (Figure 7.2), it will tend to move in some direction lying within the angle RPQ. So that, unless some external event should arise to disturb the trade relations between the two countries, the exchange-index must soon strike either OE between Q and A, or OG between R and A. But, as we cannot tell the relative magnitude of the horizontal tendency along PQ, and of the vertical tendency along PR we cannot predict which of the two curves it will strike first. Suppose it strike OE first: when it is on OE there will be no force tending to make it move either to the right or to the left. But there will be a force attracting it upwards. It will therefore tend to oscillate along QA towards A. For we may use this brief phrase to express the fact that the exchange-index will not necessarily remain on QA during the whole of its motion to A but may oscillate first on one side of QA and then on the other:

---

[1]Thus the motion of the exchange-index is in every respect similar to that of a material particle moving freely under the action of forces which attract it towards OE and OG. Suppose OE to be a rigid wire which exerts attractions only in a horizontal direction and always towards the right when the particle is, according to the definition in the text, on the left of OE, and vice versa. Similarly suppose OG to be a rigid wire which exerts attractions only in a vertical direction, and always upwards when the particle is, according to the definition in the text, below OG, and vice versa. Then this particle will move exactly in the same manner as does our exchange-index, so that if we chose to assign to these horizontal and vertical forces any particular laws we should obtain a differential equation for the motion of the exchange-index. This equation when integrated would give us the path which on this particular supposition the particle would describe. Such calculations might afford considerable scope to the ingenuity or those who devise mathematical problems, but as we shall see ... they would afford no aid to the Economist.

under the action of the forces which urge it to the right whenever it is to the left of OE, and to the left whenever it is to the right of OE. It will, however, unless its movements be disturbed by some powerful cause extraneous to the ordinary circumstances of the trade, in general adhere somewhat closely to QA. It will be convenient also to place at each of several points on the curve an arrowhead, to indicate the direction in which the exchange-index, if at that point would be made to oscillate along the curve on which it is by the force exerted on it by the other curve. Similarly, if the exchange-index moving from P had struck the curve OG first it would have oscillated along RA towards A.

Exactly in the same way it may be proved that if the exchange-index were at any time at P' it would be impelled by the forces acting on it to move upwards to the left: that if it struck OE first it would oscillate along QA towards A; and that if it struck OG first it would oscillate along GA towards A. And similarly for the points P'' and p'''.

Finally, if the exchange-index coming towards A shoot beside it or beyond it in any direction, or if the exchange-index be displaced by any disturbing event from A in any direction, the forces acting upon it will bring it back to OE or OG, and cause it to oscillate along that curve which it strikes first toward A.

It will be convenient to speak of the equilibrium of the trade between England and Germany corresponding to a point of intersection of OE and OG as the equilibrium at that point. We may now give a formal

DEFINITION. The equilibrium at a point of intersection of OE and OG is *stable*, provided that when the exchange-index strikes either of the curves in the neighbourhood of that point, the forces acting on the index tend to make it oscillate along the curve *towards* that point. In other cases the equilibrium is *unstable*.

It will be seen hereafter that the equilibrium at every point in which OE and OC cut one another, if it is unstable for displacements in any direction, is unstable for displacements in every direction. But this result does not hold of points in which the curves meet but touch without cutting one another.

We may now enunciate the fundamental rule for deciding whether any

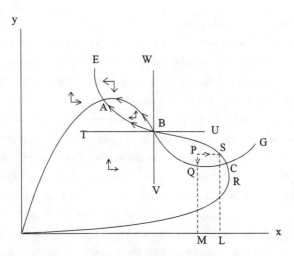

Figure 7.3: Unstable Equilibria

particular point of intersection of the curves corresponds to a stable or to an unstable equilibrium of the trade. But, in order that this may be given in a convenient form, it is necessary to have some handy means of distinguishing the various directions in which different parts of the curves may lie.

If a point moves from O along OE in Figure 7.3, it at first increases its distance from Oy at the same time that it increases its distance from Ox. It continues to do so until it arrives at R when the direction of the curve is vertical. If the point continues its motion from R onwards to C and B, it will continue to recede, but it will approach towards Oy. It will be convenient to express the difference between the portions of OE by saying that between O and R the curve is inclined *positively*; and that from R to B, and for some distance beyond B, the curve is inclined *negatively*. Or more generally:

Whatever portion of a curve lies in such a direction that a point, which moves along it so as to recede from Ox, recedes also from Oy; that portion of the curve is said to be *inclined positively*. Conversely, whatever portion of a curve lies in such a direction that a point which moves along it so as to recede from Ox approaches Oy; that portion or the curve is said to be *inclined negatively*.

Using these terms we may enunciate

PROP. XII. *The equilibrium is stable at every point of intersection of OE and OG, excepting those at which both curves are inclined positively, but OG is more nearly vertical than OE, and excepting those at which both curves are inclined negatively, but OG is more nearly vertical than OE.*

In accordance with this Proposition, the equilibria at A and C in [Figure 7.3] are stable, and the equilibrium at B in each of these figures is unstable, as has been already indicated. The most convenient mode of establishing this Proposition is perhaps to draw a number of figures representative of every position in which the curves can lie at a point of intersection. Arrow-heads should then be inserted to indicate in conformity with Prop. XI, the directions of the forces which would act upon the exchange-index at different points in the figures, so as to exhibit the motion of the exchange-index.

If through B in Figure 7.3 there be drawn the straight lines TBU from left to right, and VBW vertically upwards, then if the exchange-point be displaced to a position within the quadrant TBW, it will tend to move to A. If displaced to a position within the quadrant VBU it will tend to move to C. If displaced to a position in either of the quadrants TBV, WBU, it will tend to move to A or C, according to whether the forces acting upon it bring it into the quadrant TBW, or into the quadrant VBU. In this last case it is just possible that the exchange-index may on its way back strike B. This possibility is worthy of note. But the motion of the exchange-index is not likely to be arrested at B; and if disturbed from B ever so little along either of the curves it would tend to move off to A or C. Therefore it is not inaccurate to describe the equilibrium at B as unstable. Indeed precisely analogous cases occur in Mechanics. A body displaced from equilibrium may pass through a position of unstable equilibrium on its way towards a position of stable equilibrium.

The Appendix on Barter

In an article in the *Giornale degli Economisti* for February, 1891, Prof Edgeworth draws the adjoining diagram [Figure 7.4], which represents the cases of barter of apples for nuts ... Apples are measured along Ox, and nuts along Oy; $Op = 4$, $pa = 40$, and a represents the termination of the first bargain in which 4 apples have been exchanged for 40 nuts, in the case in which A gets the advantage at starting: b represents the second, and c the final stage of that case. On the other hand, a' represents the first, and b', c', d' the second, third and final stages of the set of bargains in which B gets the advantage at starting. QP, the locus on which c and d' must both necessarily lie, is called by Prof. Edgeworth the *Contract Curve*. Following a method adopted in his *Mathematical Psychics* (1881), he takes U to represent the total utility to A of apples and nuts when he has given up x apples and received y nuts, V the total utility to B of apples and nuts when he has received x apples and given up y nuts. If an additional Δx apples are exchanged for Δy nuts, the exchange will be indifferent to A if

$$\frac{dU}{dx}\Delta x + \frac{dU}{dy}\Delta y = 0 \cdot$$

and it will be indifferent to B if $\frac{dV}{dx}\Delta x + \frac{dV}{dy}\Delta y = 0$. These, therefore, are the equations to the indifference curves OP and OQ of the figures respectively; and the contract curve which is the locus of points at which the terms of exchange that are indifferent to A are also indifferent to B has the elegant equation $\frac{dU}{dx} \div \frac{dU}{dy} = \frac{dV}{dx} \div \frac{dV}{dy}$.

If the marginal utility of nuts be constant for A and also for B, $\frac{dU}{dy}$ and $\frac{dV}{dy}$ become constant; U becomes $\Phi(a-x) + \alpha y$, and V becomes $\Psi(a-x) + \beta y$; and the contract curve becomes $F(x) = o$; $x = C$; that is, it is a straight line parallel to Oy, and the value of $\Delta y : \Delta x$ given by either of the indifference curves, a function of C; thus showing that by whatever route the barter may have started, equilibrium will have been found at a point at which C apples have been exchanged, and the final rate of exchange is a function of C' that is, it is a constant also. This last application of Prof. Edgeworth's

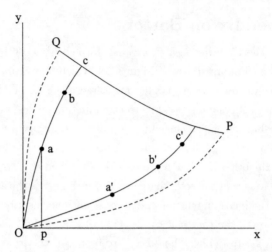

Figure 7.4: Disequilibrium Trading

mathematical version of the theory of barter, to confirm the results reached in the text, was first made by Mr Berry, and is published in the *Giornale degli Economisti* for June, 1891.

Prof. Edgeworth's plan of representing U and V as general function of x and y has great attractions to the mathematician; but it seems less adapted to express the every-day facts of economic life than that of regarding, as Jevons did, the marginal utilities of apples as functions of x simply. In that case, if A had no nuts at starting, as is assumed in the particular case under discussion, U takes the form

$$\int_0^x \phi_1 (a - x) \, d + \int_0^y \psi_1 (y) \, dy$$

similarly for V. And then the equation to the contract curve is of the form

$$\phi_1 (a - x) \div \psi_1 (y) = \phi_2 (x) \div \psi_2 (b - y)$$

which is one of the Equations of Exchange in Jevons' *Theory*, 2nd Edition, p.108.

7.2 Edgeworth

This section contains material from Edgeworth (1881, pp.17-39), where he introduces indifference curves and the contract curves, and examines the role of the number of traders.

Mathematical Psychics

Economical Calculus

DEFINITIONS. The first principle of Economics is that every agent is actuated only by self-interest. The workings of this principle may be viewed under two aspects, according as the agent acts *without*, or *with*, the consent of others affected by his actions. In wide senses, the first species of action may be called *war*; the second, *contract*. Examples: (1) A general, or fencer, making moves, a dealer lowering price, *without consent of rival.* (2) A set of co-operatives (labourers, capitalists, manager) agreed *nem. con.* to distribute the joint-produce by assigning to each a *certain function* of his sacrifice. The *articles* of contract are in this case the *amount* of sacrifice to be made by each, *and the principle of distribution.*

'Is it peace or war?' asks the lover of 'Maud', of economic *competition*, and answers hastily: It is both, *pax* or *pact* between contractors during contract, *war*, when some of the contractors *without the consent of others recontract.* Thus an auctioneer having been in contact with the last bidder (to sell at such a price *if* no higher bid) *recontracts* with a higher bidder. So a landlord on expiry of lease recontracts, it may be, with a new tenant.

The *field of competition* with reference to a contract, or contracts, under consideration consists of all the individuals who are willing and able to recontract about the articles under consideration. Thus in an auction the field consists of the auctioneer and all who are effectively willing and able to recontract about the articles under consideration. Thus in an auction the field consists of the auctioneer and all who are effectively willing to give a

higher price than the last bid. In this case, as the transaction reaches determination, the field continually diminishes and ultimately vanishes. But this
is not the case in general. Suppose a great number of auctions going on at
the same point; or, what comes to the same thing, a market consisting of
an indefinite number of dealers, say Xs, in commodity x, and an indefinite
number of dealers, say Ys, in commodity y. In this case, up to the determination of equilibrium, the field continues indefinitely large. To be sure it
may be said to vanish at the position of equilibrium. But that circumstance
does not stultify the definition. Thus, if one chose to define the *field of force*
as the centres of force sensibly acting on a certain system of bodies, then in
a continuous medium of attracting matter, the field might be continually of
indefinite extent, might change as the system moved, might be said to vanish
when the system reached equilibrium.

There is free communication throughout a *normal* competitive field. You
might suppose the constituent individuals collected at a point, or connected
by telephones an ideal supposition, but sufficiently approximate to existence
or tendency for the purposes of abstract science.

A *perfect* field of competition professes in addition certain properties pe-
culiarly favourable to mathematical calculation; namely, a certain indefinite
multiplicity and *dividedness*, analogous to that *infinity* and *infinitesimality*
which facilitate so large a portion of Mathematical Physics (consider the
theory of Atoms, and all applications of the Differential Calculus). The
conditions of a *perfect* field are four; the first pair referrible to the heading
multiplicity or continuity, the second to *dividedness* or fluidity.

I. Any individual is free to *recontract* with any out of an indefinite number,
e.g., in the last example there are an indefinite number of Xs and similarly
of Ys.

II. Any individual is free to *contract* (at the same time) with an indefinite
number; *e.g.*, any X (and similarly Y) may deal with any number of Ys. This
condition combined with the first appears to involve the indefinite divisibility
of each *article* of contract (if any X deal with an indefinite number of Ys he
must give each an indefinitely small portion of x); which might be erected
into a separate condition.

III. Any individual is free to *recontract* with another independently of, *without the consent* being required of, any third party, *e.g.*, there is among the Ys (and similarly among the Xs) no *combination* or precontract between two or more contractors that none of them will recontract without the consent of all. Any Y then may accept the offer of any X irrespectively of other Ys.

IV. Any individual is free to *contract* with another independently of a third party; *e.g.*, in simple exchange each contract is between two only, but *secus* in the entangled contract described in the [above] example, where it may be a condition of production that there should be three at least to each bargain.

There will be observed a certain similarity between the relation of the first to the second condition, and that of the third to the fourth. The failure of the first involves the failure of the second, but not *vice versa*; and the third and fourth are similarly related.

A *settlement* is a contract which cannot be varied with the consent of all the parties to it.

A *final settlement* is a settlement which cannot be varied by recontract within the field of competition.

Contract is *indeterminate* when there are an indefinite number of *final settlements*.

The PROBLEM to which attention is specially directed in this introductory summary is: *How far contract is indeterminate* – an inquiry of more than theoretical importance, if it show not only that indeterminateness tends to be present widely, but also in what direction an escape from its evils is to be sought.

DEMONSTRATIONS. The general answer is – (α) Contract without competition is indeterminate, (β) Contract with *perfect* competition is perfectly determinate, (γ) Contract with more or less perfect competition is less or more indeterminate.

(α) Let us commence with almost the simplest case of contract, – two individuals, X and Y, whose interest depends on two variable quantities, which they are agreed not to vary without mutual consent. Exchange of two commodities is a particular case of this kind of contract. Let x and y be the portions interchanged, as in Professor Jevons's example. Then the utility of one party, say X, may be written $\Phi_1 (a - x) + \Psi_1 (y)$; and the utility of the other party, say Y, $\Phi_2 (x) + \Psi_2 (b - y)$; where Φ and Ψ are the integrals of Professor Jevons's symbols ϕ and ψ. It is agreed that x and y shall be varied only by consent (not *e.g.* by violence).

More generally. Let P, the utility of X, one party, $= F(x, y)$, and Π, the utility of Y, the other party, $= \Phi (x, y)$. If now it is inquired at what point they will reach equilibrium, one or both refusing to move further, to what *settlement* they will consent; the answer is in general that contract by itself does not supply sufficient conditions to determine the solution; supplementary conditions as will appear being supplied by competition or ethical motives, Contract will supply only one condition (for the two variables), namely

$$\frac{dP}{dx}\frac{d\Pi}{dy} = \frac{dP}{dy}\frac{d\Pi}{dx}$$

(corresponding to Professor Jevons's equation

$$\frac{\phi_1 (a - x)}{\psi_1 (y)} = \frac{\phi_2 (x)}{\psi_2 (b - y)}$$

Theory p.108), which it is proposed here to investigate.

Consider $P - F(x, y) = 0$ as a surface, P denoting the length of the ordinate drawn from any point on the plane of x, y (say the plane of the paper) to the surface. Consider $\Pi - \Phi (x, y)$ similarly. It is required to find a point (x, y) such that, *in whatever direction* we take an infinitely small step, P and Π do not increase together, but that, while one increases, the other decreases. It may be shown from a variety of points of view that the locus of the required point is

$$\frac{dP}{dx}\frac{d\Pi}{dy} - \frac{dP}{dy}\frac{d\Pi}{dx} = 0$$

which locus it is here proposed to call the *contract curve*.

(1) Consider first in what directions X can take an indefinitely small step, say of length ρ, from any point (x, y). Since the addition to P is

$$\rho \left[\left(\frac{dP}{dx} \right) \cos \theta + \left(\frac{dP}{dy} \right) \sin \theta \right]$$

$\rho \cos \theta$ being $= dx$, and $\rho \sin \theta = dy$, it is evident that X will step only on one side of a certain line, the *line of indifference*, as it might be called; its equation being

$$(\zeta - x) \left(\frac{dP}{dx} \right) + (\eta - y) \left(\frac{dP}{dy} \right) = 0$$

and it is to be observed, in passing, that the direction in which X will *prefer* to move, the line of force or *line of preference*, as it may be termed, is perpendicular to the line of indifference. Similar remarks apply to Π. If then we enquire in what directions X and Y will consent to move *together*, the answer is, in any direction between their respective lines of indifference, in a direction *positive* as it may be called *for both*. At what point then will they refuse to move at all? When their *lines of indifference* are coincident (and *lines of preference* not only coincident, but in opposite directions); whereof the *necessary* (but *not sufficient*) condition is

$$\left(\frac{dP}{dx} \right) \left(\frac{d\Pi}{dy} \right) - \left(\frac{dP}{dy} \right) \left(\frac{d\Pi}{dx} \right) = 0$$

(2) The same consideration might be thus put. Let the complete variation of P be $DP = \rho \left[\left(\frac{dP}{dx} \right) \cos \theta + \left(\frac{dP}{dy} \right) \sin \theta \right]$ and similarly for Π. Then in general θ can be taken, so that $\frac{DP}{D\Pi}$ should be positive, say $= g^2$, and so P and Π both increase together.

$$\tan \theta = \frac{\frac{dP}{dx} - g^2 \frac{d\Pi}{dx}}{\frac{dP}{dy} - g^2 \frac{d\Pi}{dy}}$$

But this solution fails when

$$\frac{\left(\frac{dP}{dx} \right)}{\left(\frac{dP}{dy} \right)} = \frac{\left(\frac{d\Pi}{dx} \right)}{\left(\frac{d\Pi}{dy} \right)}$$

In fact, in this case $\frac{DP}{D\Pi}$ *is the same for all directions.*

If, then, that common value of $\frac{DP}{D\Pi}$ is *negative*, motion is impossible in any direction.

(3) Or, again, we may consider that motion is possible so long as, one party not losing, the other gains. The point of equilibrium, therefore, may be described as a *relative maximum*, the point at which *e.g.* Π being constant,

P is a maximum. Put $P = P - c\,(\Pi - \Pi')$, where c is a constant and Π' is the supposed given value of Π. Then P is a maximum only when

$$dx \left(\frac{dP}{dx} - c\frac{d\Pi}{dx} \right) + dy \left(\frac{dP}{dy} - c\frac{d\Pi}{dy} \right) = 0;$$

whence we have as before the *contract-curve.* ...

(4) Upon the hypothesis above shadowed forth, human action generally, and in particular the step taken by a contractor modifying articles of contract, may be regarded as the working of a gross force *governed*, let on, and directed by a more delicate pleasure-force. From which it seems to follow upon general dynamical principles applied to this special case that equilibrium is attained when the *total pleasure-energy of the contractors is a maximum relative* or subject, to conditions; the conditions being here (i) that the pleasure-energy of X and Y considered each as a function of (certain values of) the variables x and y should be functions of the *same* values: in the metaphorical language above employed that the charioteer-pleasures should drive their teams *together*, over the plane of xy; (ii) that the joint team should never be urged in a direction contrary to the *preference* of either individual; that the resultant line of force (and the momentum) of the gross, the chariot, system should be continually intermediate between the (positive directions of the) lines of the respective pleasure-forces. [We may without disadvantage make abstraction of sensible momentum, and suppose thereby the condition joint system to move towards equilibrium along a line of resultant gross force. Let it start from the origin. And let us employ an *arbitrary function* to denote the unknown *principle of compromise* between the parties; suppose the ratio of the sines of angles made by the resultant line with the respective lines of pleasure-force.] Then, by reasoning different from the preceding only in the point of view, it appears that the *total utility of the system is a relative maximum at any point on the pure contract-curve.* ...

The preceding theory may easily be extended to several persons and several variables. Let $P_1 = F_1\,(x, y, z)$, denote the utility of one of three parties, utility depending on three variables, x, y, z; and similarly $P_2 = F_2$, $P_3 = F_3$. Then the *contract-settlement*, the arrangement for the alteration of which *the consent of all three parties* cannot be obtained, will be (subject to reservations analogous to those analysed in the preceding paragraphs) *the Eliminant.*

$$\frac{dP_1}{dx} \quad \frac{dP_1}{dy} \quad \frac{dP_1}{dz}$$

$$\frac{dP_2}{dx} \quad \frac{dP_2}{dy} \quad \frac{dP_2}{dz}$$

$$\frac{dP_3}{dx} \quad \frac{dP_3}{dy} \quad \frac{dP_3}{dz}$$

In general let there be m contractors and n subjects of contract, n variables. Then by the principle (3) the state of equilibrium may be considered as such that the utility of any one contractor must be a maximum *relative* to the utilities of the other contractors being constant, or not decreasing; which may be thus mathematically expressed:

$D\left(l_1 P_1 + l_2 P_2 + \&c. + l_m P_m\right) = 0$, where D represents complete increment and l_1 l_2 $\&c.$, are indeterminate multipliers; whence, if there be n variables $x_1 x_2 \ldots x_n$, we have n equations of the form

$$l_1 \frac{dP_1}{dx_1} + l_2 \frac{dP_2}{dx_1} + \&c. + l_m \frac{dP_m}{dx_1} = 0$$

from which, if n be not less than m, we can eliminate the $(m-1$ independent) constants l and obtain the contract-system consisting of $n - (m-1)$ equations.

The case of n being less than m may be sufficiently illustrated by a particular example. Let the abscissa x represent the single variable on which the utilities P and Π of two persons contracting depend. Then if p and π are the maximum points for the respective pleasure-curves ... it is evident that the tract of abscissa between π and p is of the nature of pure contract-curve; that the index being placed anywhere in that tract will be immovable; *secus* on either side beyond π and p. Similarly it may be shown that, if three individuals are in contract about two variables x y, the contract locus or region is (the space within) a curvilinear triangle in the plane x y bounded by the three contract-curves presented by successively supposing each pair of individuals to be in contract with respect to x and y. And similarly for larger numbers in hyperspace.

It is not necessary for the purpose of the present study to carry the analysis further. To gather up and fix our thoughts, let us imagine a simple case – Robinson Crusoe contracting with Friday. The *articles* of contract: wages to be given by the white, labour to be given by the black. Let Robinson Crusoe $= X$. Represent y, the labour given by Friday, by a horizontal line measured *northward* from an assumed point, and measure x, the remuneration given by Crusoe, from the same point along an *eastward* line (See accompanying figure 7.5). Then any point between these lines represents a contract. It will very generally be the interest of both parties to vary the articles of any contract taken at random. But there is a class of contracts to the variation of which the consent of *both* parties cannot be obtained, *of settlements.* These settlements are represented by an *indefinite number* of points, a locus, the *contract-curve CC'*, or rather, a certain portion of it which may be supposed to be wholly in the space between our perpendicular lines in a direction trending, from south-east to northwest. This available portion of the contract-curve lies between two points, say $\eta_0 x_0$ north-west, and $y_0 \xi_0$ south-east; which are respectively the intersections with the contract-curve of the *curves of indifference* for each party drawn through the origin. Thus the utility of the contract represented by $\eta_0 x_0$ is for Friday zero, or rather, the same as if there was no contract. At that point he would as soon be off with the bargain – work by himself perhaps.

This simple case brings clearly into view the characteristic evil of indeterminate contract, *deadlock*, undecidable opposition of interests, ἀκριτός ἔρις καὶ ταραχή [increasing strife and disturbance]. It is the interest of both parties that there should be *some settlement*, one of the contracts represented by the contract-curve between the limits. But *which* of these contracts is arbitrary in the absence of arbitration, the interests of the two *adversa pugnantia fronte* [fighting face to face] all along the contract-curve, Y desiring to get as far as possible south-east towards $y_0 \xi_0$, X north-west toward $\eta_0 r_0$. And it further appears from the preceding analysis that in the case of any number of *articles* (for instance, Robinson Crusoe to give Friday in the way of Industrial Partnership a fraction of the produce as well as wages, or again, *arrangements about the mode* of work), the *contract-locus* may still be rep-

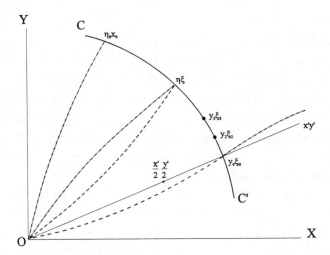

Figure 7.5: The Contract Curve

resented as a sort of line, along which the pleasure-forces of the contractors are mutually antagonistic.

An accessory evil of indeterminate contract is the tendency, greater than in a full market, towards dissimulation and objectionable arts of higgling. As Professor Jevons says with reference to a similar case, 'Such a transaction must be settled upon other than strictly economical grounds ... The art of bargaining consists in the buyer ascertaining the lowest price at which the seller is willing to part with his object, without disclosing, if possible, the highest price which he, the buyer, is willing to give'. Compare Courcelle-Seneuil's account of the contract between a hunter and a woodman in an isolated region.

With this clogged and underground procedure is contrasted (β) the smooth machinery of the open market. As Courcelle-Seneuil says, 'à mesure que le nombre des concurrents augmente, les conditions d'échange deviennent plus nécessaires, plus impersonelles en quelque sorte'. You might suppose each dealer to write down his *demand,* how much of an article he would take at each price, without attempting to conceal his requirements; and these data having been furnished to a sort of market-machine, the *price* to be passionlessly evaluated.

That contract in a state of perfect competition is determined by demand and supply is generally accepted, but is hardly to be fully understood without mathematics. The mathematics of a perfect market have been worked out by several eminent writers, in particular Messrs. Jevons, Marshall, Walras; to whose varied cultivation of the mathematical science, *Catallactics*, the reader is referred who wishes to dig down to the root of first principles, to trace out all the branches of a complete system, to gather fruits rare and only to be reached by a mathematical substructure.

There emerges amidst the variety of construction and terminology πολλῶν ὀνομάτων μορφὴ μία [one shape with many names], an essentially identical graphical form or analytical formula expressing the equation of supply to demand; whereof the simplest type, the catallactic molecule, as it might be called, is presented in the case above described in the definition of perfect competition.[2] The familiar pair of equations is deduced by the present writer from the first principle: Equilibrium is attained when the existing contracts can neither be varied without recontract with the consent of the existing parties, nor by recontract within the field of competition. The advantage of this general method is that it is applicable to the particular cases of imperfect competition; where the conceptions of *demand and supply at a price* are no longer appropriate.

The catallactic molecule is compounded, when we suppose the Xs and Ys dealing in respect each of *several* articles with several sets of Zs, As, Bs, &c.; a case resolved by M. Walras.

Thus the actual commercial field might be represented by sets of entrepreneurs Xs, Ys, Zs, each X buying labour from among sets of labourers, As, Bs, Cs, use of capital from among sets of capitalists, Js, Ks, Ls, use of land from among sets of landowners, Ps, Qs, Rs, and selling products among a set of consumers consisting of the sum of the three aforesaid classes *and* the entrepreneurs of a species different from X, the Ys and Zs. As the demand

---

[2] ... It must be carefully remembered that Prof. Jevons's Formulae of Exchange apply not to bare individuals, an isolated couple, but (as he himself sufficiently indicates, p.98), to individuals clothed with the properties of a market, a typical couple. The isolated couple, the catallactic *atom*, would obey our (*a*) law.

of the labourer is deducible from considering his utility as a function of wages received and work done, so the demand of the entrepreneur is deducible from considering his utility as a function of (1) his expenditures on the agents of production; (2) his expenditures in the way of consumption; (3) his receipts from sale of produce; (4) his labour of superintendence. The last-named variable is not an article of contract; But there being supposed a definite relation connecting the produce with agents of production and entrepreneur's labour, the catallactic formulae become applicable. This is a very abstract representation (abstracting *e.g.* risk, foreign trade, the migration from one employment to another, *e.g.* Xs becoming Ys, &c.), yet more concrete than that of M. Walras, who apparently makes the more abstract supposition of a sort of *frictionless* entrepreneur, 'faisant ni perte ni bénéfice'. ...

But it is not the purport of the present study to attempt a detailed, much less a polemical, discussion of pure Catallactics, but rather (γ) to inquire how far contract is determinate in cases of imperfect competition. It is not necessary for this purpose to attack the *general problem of Contract qualified by Competition*, which is much more difficult than the general problem of unqualified contract already treated. It is not necessary to resolve analytically the composite mechanism of a *competitive field*. It will suffice to proceed synthetically, observing in a simple typical case the effect of continually introducing into the field additional competitors.

1. Let us start, then, from the abstract typical case above put an X and Y dealing respectively in x and y. Here x represents the *sacrifice objectively measured* of X; it may be manual work done, or commodity manufactured, or capital abstained from during a certain time. And y is the objectively measured remuneration of X. Hence it may be assumed, according to the two first axioms of the Utilitarian Calculus, the law of increasing labour, and the law of decreasing utility, that P being the utility of X, (1) $\frac{dP}{dx}$ is continually *negative*, $\frac{dP}{dy}$ *positive*; (2) $\frac{d_2P}{dx^2}$, $\frac{d_2P}{dy^2}$, $\frac{d_2P}{dxdy}$, continually *negative*. (Attention is solicited to the interpretation of the third condition.) No doubt these latter conditions are subject to many exceptions, especially in regard to abstinence from capital, and in case of purchase not for consumption, but with a view to re-sale; and in the sort of cases comprised in Mr. Marshall's Class II. curves.

Still, these exceptions, though they destroy the watertightness of many of the reasonings in this and the companion calculus, are yet perhaps of secondary importance to one taking a general abstract view.

This being premised, let us now introduce a second X and a second Y; so that the field of competition consists of two Xs and two Ys. And for the sake of illustration (not of the argument) let us suppose that the new X has the same requirements, the same nature as the old X; and similarly that the new Y is equal natured with the old.

Then it is evident that there cannot be equilibrium unless (1) all the field is collected at one point; (2) that point is on the *contract-curve*. For (1) if possible let one couple be at one point, and another couple at another point. It will generally be the interest of the X of one couple and the Y of the other to rush together, leaving their partners in the lurch. And (2) if the common point is not on the contract-curve, it will be the interest of *all parties* to descend to the contract-curve.

The points of the contract-curve in the immediate neighbourhood of the limits $y_0\xi_0$ and $\eta_0 x_0$ cannot be *final settlements*. For if the system be placed at such a point, say slightly north-west of $y_0\xi_0$, it will in general be possible for *one* of the Ys (without the consent of the other) to recontract with the two Xs, so that for all those three parties the *recontract* is more advantageous than the previously existing contract. For the right line joining the origin to (the neighbourhood of) $y_0\xi_0$ will in general lie altogether within the *indifference curve* drawn from the origin to $y_0\xi_0$. For the indifference-curve is in general convex to the abscissa. For its differential equation is

$$-\frac{dy}{dx} = \frac{\left(\frac{dF(x,y)}{dx}\right)}{\left(\frac{dF(x,y)}{dy}\right)}$$

whence

$$\frac{d_2 y}{dx^2} = \frac{-\left[\left(\frac{d_2 F}{dx^2}\right) + \left(\frac{d_2 F}{dx\,dy}\right)\frac{dy}{dx}\right]\left(\frac{dF}{dy}\right) + \left(\frac{dF}{dx}\right)\left[\left(\frac{d_2 F}{dx\,dy}\right) + \frac{d_2 F}{dy^2}\frac{dy}{dx}\right]}{\left(\frac{dF}{dy}\right)^2}$$

which is perfectly *positive*. Therefore the indifference-curve (so far as we are concerned with it) is convex to the abscissa.

Now, at the contract-curve the two indifference-curves for X and Y *touch.*
Thus the figure 7.5 is proved to be a correct representation, indicating that
a point $x'y'$ can be found both more advantageous for Y than the point
on the contract-curve $y_1\xi_1$ (on an *interior* indifference-curve, as it may be
said), and also such that its co-ordinates are the sums (respectively) of the
co-ordinates of two other points, both more advantageous for an X. These
latter points to be occupied by X_1, and X_2 may be properly regarded (owing
to the symmetry and competition) as *coincident*; with co-ordinates $\frac{x'}{2}, \frac{y'}{2}$.
Further, it appears from previous reasonings that there will be a *contract-*
relation between (x', y') and $\left(\frac{x'}{2}, \frac{y'}{2}\right)$; namely $\frac{\Phi'_x(x',y')}{\phi'_y(x',y')} = \dfrac{F'_x\left(\frac{x'}{2}, \frac{y'}{2}\right)}{F'_y\left(\frac{x'}{2}, \frac{y'}{2}\right)}$; where F'_x
is put for the first partially derived function $\left(\frac{dF(x,y)}{dx}\right)$

When this relation is satisfied the system of three might remain in the
position reached; but for Y_2 who has been left out in the cold. He will now
strike in, with the result that the system will be worked down to the contract-
curve again; to a point at least as favourable for the Xs as $\frac{x'}{2}, \frac{y'}{2}$. Thus the Ys
will have lost some of their original advantage by competition. And a certain
process of which this is an abstract typical representation will go on as long
as it is possible to find point x' y' with the requisite properties. Attention to
the problem will show that the process will come to a stop at a point on the
contract-curve $y_2\xi_2$, such that if a line joining it to the origin intersect the
curve, the *supplementary contract-curve* as it might be called,

$$\frac{\Phi'_x(x,y)}{\Phi'_y(x,y)} = \frac{F'_x\left(\frac{x}{2}, \frac{y}{2}\right)}{F'_y\left(\frac{x}{2}, \frac{y}{2}\right)}$$

in the point x', y' then $\Phi(\xi_2, y_2) = \Phi(x', y')$, *provided that* $\left(\frac{x'}{2}, \frac{y'}{2}\right)$ falls within
the indifference-curve for Y drawn through $(\xi_2 y_2)$. If otherwise, a slightly
different system of equations must be employed.

If now a *third* X and third Y (still equal-natured) be introduced into
the field, the system can be worked down to a point $\xi_3 y_3$; whose conditions
are obtained from those just written by substituting for $\frac{x'}{2}$ $\frac{y'}{2}$, $\frac{2x'}{3}$ $\frac{2y'}{3}$. For
this represents the last point at which 2 Ys can recontract with 3 Xs with
advantage to all five. Analytical geometry will show that this point is lower

down (in respect of the advantage of Y) than $\xi_2 y_2$. In the limit, when the Xs and Ys are indefinitely (equally) multiplied, we shall have (x', y') coincident with (ξ_∞, y_∞), or as we may say for convenience (ξ, η), satisfying one or other of the *alternatives* corresponding to those just mentioned.

In case of the first alternative we have

$$\xi \Phi'_x (\xi, \eta) + \eta \Phi'_y (\xi, \eta) = 0$$

For

$$\Phi(\xi, \eta) = \Phi(x', y') = \Phi((1 + h) \xi (1 + h) \eta)$$

In the limiting case h is infinitesimal. Whence by differentiating the above equation is obtained. And the second alternative ($\frac{x'}{2}, \frac{y'}{2}$ *not* falling on the indifference-curve of Y) is not to be distinguished from the first in the limiting case.

If this reasoning does not seem satisfactory, it would be possible to give a more formal proof; bringing out the important result that the common tangent to both indifference-curves at the point ξ η is the vector from the origin.

By a parity of reasoning it may be shown that, if the system had been started at the north-west extremity of (the available portion of) the contract-curve, it would have been worked down by competition *between the Xs* to the same point; determined by the intersection with the contract-curve of $\xi F'_x + \eta F'_y = 0$; for the *same* point is determined by the intersection of *either* curve with the contract-curve. For the three curves evidently intersect in the same point.

Taking account of the two processes which have been described, the competing Ys being worked down for a certain distance towards the north-west, and similarly the competing Xs towards the south-east: we see that in general for any number short of the *practically infinite* (if such a term be allowed) there is a finite length of contract-curve, from $\xi_m y_m$ to $x_m \eta_m$, at any point of which if the system is placed, it cannot by contract or recontract be displaced; that there are *an indefinite number of final settlements*, a quantity continually diminishing as we approach a perfect market. We are brought back again to case (β), on which some further remarks have been conveniently postponed to this place. ...

The two conditions, $\xi\Phi'_x + \eta\Phi'_y = 0$ and $\xi F'_x + \eta F'_y = 0$, just obtained correspond to Professor Jevons's two equations of exchange. His formulae are to be regarded as representing the transactions of two *individuals in, or subject to, the law of, a market*. Our assumed *unity of nature* in the midst of plurality of persons naturally brings out the same result. The represented two curves may be called *demand curves*, as each expresses the amount of dealing which will afford to one of the dealers the maximum of advantage *at a certain rate of exchange a value of* $\frac{y}{x}$. This might be elegantly expressed in polar co-ordinates, $\tan\theta$ will then be the rate of exchange, and, if P be the utility of X, $\left(\frac{dP}{d\rho}\right) = 0$ is the demand-curve. By a well known property of analysis $\left(\frac{dP}{d\rho}\right) = 0$ represents not only maximum points, but *minimum points*; the lowest depths of valley, as well as the highest elevations, which one moving continually in a fixed right line from the origin over the *utility-surface* would reach.

Chapter 8

Later Expositions

8.1 Launhardt

*This section contains material from Launhardt (1993, pp.33-45), first pub-
lished in 1885. Here he examines the nature of supply and demand curves,
along with the gains from trade and trading at disequilibrium prices.*

Mathematical Principles of Economics
The Fundamental Law of Barter

If an owner of good A, the utility function of which is $y = F(x)$, owns a
quantity a, and another owner of good B with a utility function of $y = \Phi(z)$,
owns a quantity b, those two owners can exchange a certain quantity of their
goods with each other and will do this to the extent to which they derive
utility. Initially it may be supposed that the utility of both goods is estimated
by the owners to be equal, in other words the value of the goods is based by
both owners on the utility function for good A of $y = F(x)$ and for good B
of $y = \Phi(z)$.

　　If in barter, p'' units of good A are exchanged for p' units of good B, with
x units of good A which are bartered for z units of good B, the result must
be $z = (p'/p'')x$. The relative values p' and p'' on which the barter is based
are obviously nothing but the unit prices p' for good A and p'' for good B
measured on some sort of scale.

　　After the exchange the owner of A has retained of his initial good an
amount $a - x$ and of the other good a quantity z, so that the utility of his

possession is as follows:

$$N = F(a - x) + \Phi(z)$$

The value of x for which utility is a maximum is found by differentiating with respect to x and setting the result equal to zero. This gives: $-F'(a - x) + \Phi'(z) dz/dx = 0$, and as $z = (p'/p'') x$, $dz/dx = p'/p''$ and:

$$\frac{F'(a - x)}{\Phi'(z)} = \frac{p'}{p''} \qquad (8.1)$$

The Fundamental Law of Barter derives from this equation, which expressed in words is as follows: *For an owner the highest degree of utility of an exchange of goods is reached if the degrees of utility of the goods in his possession relate as do unit prices of the goods.*

Equation (8.1) can also be expressed as:

$$\frac{F'(a - x)}{p'} = \frac{\Phi'(z)}{p''} \qquad (8.2)$$

If one names the quotient of the degree of utility and the unit price the *priceworthiness* of the goods, then the fundamental law of barter can be expressed in the following manner: *For the owner, equality of priceworthiness must be achieved through an exchange of the goods in his possession.*

The correctness of this sentence can be understood without mathematical argument by simple reflection. The priceworthiness of goods indicates the degree of utility per unit price. If this measure were less for one of the goods than for the other, one would gain in pleasure if further quantities of the good for which the unit price gives less utility were exchanged for further quantities of the good which gives greater pleasure per unit price. The limit for the continuation of the exchange will be reached as soon as the degree of utility of both goods relative to the price per unit will be received.

For the second owner B the same conditions apply. He will have reached, after the exchange, a utility from his possessions which is equal to:

$$N = \Phi(b - x) + F(x)$$

By differentiating with respect to z the condition for the maximum is:
$-\Phi'(b-z)+F'(x)\,dx/dz=0$, and as $dx/dz=p''/p'$:

$$\frac{F'(x)}{\Phi'(b-x)}=\frac{p'}{p''} \tag{8.3}$$

or

$$\frac{F'(x)}{p'}=\frac{\Phi'(b-z)}{p''} \tag{8.4}$$

However, the second owner will not always value goods A and B according to the same utility function as the first owner. If he estimates the utility of good A on $y=F(y)$ and the utility of good B not on $y=\Phi(z)$, but on $y=\psi(z)$, then the fundamental law of barter will be to him:

$$\frac{F'(x)}{\psi'(b-z)}=\frac{p'}{p''}$$

thus the same fundamental law of barter applies.

Supply of Goods

If from equation (8.1) which for the owner of good A offers the most favourable conditions for the barter against good B, x is obtained the extent of *supply* is derived, that is the quantity of the goods which an owner at a given relative price of p'/p'' has to exchange of his own possessions to derive a maximum of utility. If the relative price on which the exchange is based changes, the supply will also change. Supply is therefore a function of price which is demonstrated in Figure 8.1 which shows the relative prices as abscissas and the corresponding values of supply as ordinates.

Supply will be zero if the price of the offered good A is reduced to p^0, which is given by:

$$\frac{F'(a)}{\Phi(0)}=\frac{p^0}{p''}$$

Only after the price of good A available for exchange rises above the price, p^0, will the owner of A wish to exchange a quantity of his good, given in (8.1), for good B. This supply increases with the price p' until at a certain price a maximum supply is reached, because with a further increase in price the owner of A will receive a quantity of good B so large that a maximum of

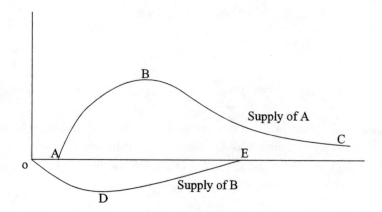

Figure 8.1: Supply Curves

satisfaction is reached after only a small quantity of his highly priced good is made available. The graph of supply in Figure 8.1, depicted as the curve ABC, approaches the abscissa asymptotically from point B after having reached the maximum.

In order to obtain a more vivid idea of the shape of the *supply equation* and the *supply curve*, I shall introduce for the utility functions ...

$$F(x) = \alpha x - \alpha_1 x^2$$

and

$$\Phi(z) = \beta z - \beta_1 z^2$$

that would mean that owner A, after having exchanged x of his good A for z of good B at a price ratio of p'/p'' has reached the following utility:

$$N = \alpha(a - x) - \alpha_1(a - x)^2 + \beta x p'/p'' - \beta_1(p'/p'')^2$$

For maximum utility, differentiate with respect to x to give:

$$-\alpha + 2\alpha_1(a - x) + \beta p'/p'' - 2\beta_1 x(p'/p'')^2 = 0$$

from which the supply becomes:

$$x = \frac{\beta p'/p'' - (\alpha - 2\alpha_1 a)}{2\left(\alpha_1 + \beta_1(p'/p'')^2\right)} \qquad (8.5)$$

This supply will be zero for

$$p'/p'' = (\alpha - 2\alpha_1 a)/\beta \tag{8.6}$$

and the maximum for

$$\frac{p'}{p''} = \frac{\alpha - 2\alpha_1 a}{\beta} + \left\{ \left(\frac{\alpha - 2\alpha_1 a}{\beta} \right)^2 + \frac{\alpha_1}{\beta_1} \right\}^{0.5} \tag{8.7}$$

Equation (8.6) can also be expressed as:

$$\frac{\beta}{p''} = \frac{\alpha - 2\alpha_1 a}{p'}$$

As β/p'' represents the priceworthiness of the first unit exchanged for good B, $\alpha - 2\alpha_1 a$ represents the marginal utility and therefore $(\alpha - 2\alpha_1 a)/p'$ shows the priceworthiness of the last unit of good A spent on obtaining the first unit of good B, thus the equation indicates: The supply of good A begins as soon as the priceworthiness of the last unit of this good equals the priceworthiness of the first unit of good B available for exchange. ...

For the second proprietor B conditions under which he offers his good develop much in the same way. If he has given from his supply z and exchanged it for zp''/p' of good A, so his utility is:

$$N = \beta(b - z) + \beta_1(b - z)^2 + \alpha z p''/p' - \alpha_1 z^2 (p''/p')^2$$

This becomes a maximum for:

$$z = \frac{\alpha p''/p' - (\beta - 2\beta_1 b)}{2\alpha_1 (p''/p')^2 + \beta_1}$$

or if numerator and denominator are multiplied by p'^2/p''^2:

$$z = \frac{\alpha p'/p'' - (p'/p'')^2 (\beta - 2\beta_1 b)}{2 \left(\alpha_1 + \beta_1 (p'/p'')^2 \right)} \tag{8.8}$$

Thus supplies become zero when:

$$\frac{\alpha}{p'} = \frac{\beta - 2\beta_1 b}{p''}$$

that is, if the priceworthiness of the first unit of good A to be bartered for good B corresponds to the unit of good B to be exchanged. The supply turns to zero for $p'/p'' = 0$, that is when supply is maximum, the price, p'' of good B is infinitely large compared to the price, p', of good A. ...

In Figure 8.1 supplies z are depicted according to (8.8) for various quantities of the relative price, p'/p'', of good B entered as ordinates below the axis of abscissas and represented by curve ODE.

Demand

If equation (8.3), which has established the most favourable conditions for trader B for the barter of his good A, is solved for x, one arrives at the quantity of good A which can be exchanged by trader B most favourably, that is to reach a maximum of benefit, with a price ratio of p'/p''. This is the extent of the *demand* for the good A. The demand is naturally greatest when the price p' of good A equals zero and will reach $\alpha/2\alpha_1$, when saturation develops when the degree of utility $F'(x) = 0$. The higher is the price p' compared to price p'' of good B, the smaller is the demand, until finally it is zero when:

$$\frac{p'}{p''} = \frac{F'(0)}{\Phi'(b)}$$

that is for

$$\frac{\Phi'(b)}{p''} = \frac{F'(0)}{p'}$$

when the priceworthiness of the first available unit of good A is as large as the last unit of good B available for exchange.

If demand is depicted as ordinates to the abscissa measuring the price ratio p'/p'' the locus of these ordinates determine the *demand curve* as is demonstrated in Figure 8.1 as FGH. For better demonstration we may, as in the case of the supply curve, base the demand curve on the utility function. If trader B has exchanged a quantity $z = (p'/p'')x$ of his good for x of good A he will have reached utility of

$$N = \beta\left(b - xp'/p''\right) - \beta_1\left(b - xp'/p''\right)^2 + \alpha x - \alpha_1 x^2$$

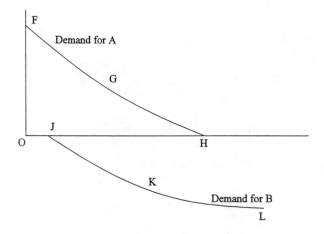

Figure 8.2: Demand Curves

which will reach a maximum for

$$x'' = \frac{\alpha - (\beta - 2\beta_1 b)\, p'/p''}{2\left\{\alpha_1 + (p'/p'')^2 /\beta_1\right\}} \tag{8.9}$$

This demand will turn to zero for

$$\frac{p'}{p''} = \frac{\alpha}{\beta - 2\beta_1 b}$$

... The demand of trader A for good B is found in the same way. If he has exchanged a quantity $x = (p''/p')\, z$ for z of good B his utility is:

$$N = \alpha\, (a - zp''/p') - \alpha_1\, (a - zp''/p')^2 + \beta z - \beta_1 z^2$$

which will reach its maximum for:

$$z'' = \frac{\beta - (p''/p')\, (\alpha - 2\alpha_1 a)}{2\left\{\alpha_1 (p''/p')^2 + \beta_1\right\}} \tag{8.10}$$

$$= \frac{\beta\, (p'/p'')^2 - (p'/p'')\, (\alpha - 2\alpha_1 a)}{2\left\{\alpha_1 + (p'/p'')^2 \beta_1\right\}} \tag{8.11}$$

The demand commences when:

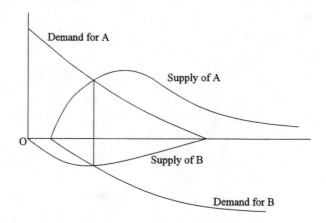

Figure 8.3: Market Equilibrium

$$\frac{p'}{p''} = \frac{\beta}{\alpha - 2\alpha_1 a}$$

and steadily increases the more p'/p'' grows, and approaches asymptotically the value $\beta/2\beta_1$, with which saturation of good B has been established. The demand curve of trader A for good B is depicted in Figure 8.2 by the line JKL ...

Equality of Supply and Demand: Equilibrium Prices

In Figure 8.3 the supply and demand curves of good A are above the abscissa and those for good B below it. If the price ratio p'/p'' is small, then the demand for the low-priced good A is large; this is however not offered at all at a low price so that no exchange can take place. Only after the price rises to $p' = (1/9)p''$ is good A offered in small quantities, and is still in strong demand but not as strongly as previously. With a growing price ratio the supply of good A increases, but the demand decreases until at a certain price ratio demand and supply will be in balance, a situation depicted at the point of intersection of the supply curve with the demand curve. In the market place the price of the good demanded will rise, as long as demand is not satisfied by supply; as soon as supply exceeds demand, a fall in the price for the good in question will occur. The battle over the price will cease only after supply and demand are equally strong. The prices resulting from such a situation are called *equilibrium prices* by Walras. The condition for equilibrium prices is reached when equations (8.1) and (8.3) coincide:

$$\frac{F'(a-x)}{\Phi'(z)} = \frac{F'(x)}{\Phi'(b-z)} \tag{8.12}$$

Equilibrium develops when equations (8.6) and (8.9) coincide, in the case of the supply and demand of goods A, or by (8.8) and (8.10) coinciding which indicate supply and demand for goods B:

$$\frac{p'}{p''} = \frac{\alpha - \alpha_1 a}{\beta - \beta_1 b} \tag{8.13}$$

. . .

Gain Through Exchange

Trader A who possessed prior to the exchange a utility $F(a)$ has obtained after the exchange a utility of $F(a-x) + \Phi(z)$; that is, utility gained by the exchange is:

$$G' = F(a-x) - F(a) + \Phi(z)$$

while the gain of trader B is as follows:

$$G'' = \Phi(b-z) - \Phi(b) + F(x)$$

Without knowledge of the form of the utility function, the extent of these gains cannot be proved. If the utility functions are based on the approximations $F(x) = \alpha x - \alpha_1 x^2$ and $\Phi(z) = \beta z - \beta_1 z^2$, then:

$$G' = \beta z - (\alpha - 2\alpha_1 a) x - \alpha_1 x^2 - \beta_1 z^2 \tag{8.14}$$

$$G'' = \alpha z - (\beta - 2\beta_1 b) z - \alpha_1 x^2 - \beta_1 z^2 \tag{8.15}$$

If $z = (p'/p'')x$, the resulting gain for both proprietors, at equilibrium prices $\frac{p'}{p''} = \frac{\alpha - \alpha_1 a}{\beta - \beta_1 b}$, if the quantity exchanged is obtained from (8.5) or (8.9) is for both:

$$G = \frac{\{a\alpha_1 (\beta - \beta_1 b) + b\beta_1 (\alpha - \alpha_1 a)\}^2}{4 \left\{\alpha_1 (\beta - \beta_1 b)^2 + \beta_1 (\alpha - \alpha_1 a)^2\right\}} \tag{8.16}$$

The truth of the statement that *in an exchange at equilibrium both owners gain equal amounts*, is only proved in the case where the utility function is of the form accepted as approximately correct. ...

8.2 Wicksell

This section contains material from Wicksell (1954, pp.53-91), first published in 1893, in which he presents the basic model of exchange and examines the gains from trade, making use of Launhardt's analysis.

The New Theory of Value
Different Uses of the Same Kind of Commodity

The simplest form of exchange is that in which the owner of a quantity of goods can and will make different uses of its different parts. The above-mentioned colonist, for example will keep for himself, his poultry and parrots only a part of his stock of corn for food purposes; the rest he will convert into spirits. It is obvious, then, that he must proportion the two parts to each other in such a way that the marginal utility on both sides becomes the same – in such a way, that is to say, that the last quantity of the remaining corn gives him the same enjoyment as the last quantity of the corn converted into spirits.

Put into an analytical form, this would be expressed as follows: The smallest enjoyment of one unit – for example, one kilogram of corn (the marginal utility of corn) – is conceived as a diminishing function of the supply which still remains after converting part of it into spirits. If, for example, the original supply consisted of a kilograms of corn, and x kilograms of it have already been converted into spirits, so that $a - x$ kilograms of corn are left, the marginal utility of corn, which was originally $F(a)$, has now risen to $F(a - x)$. In the same way the smallest enjoyment of one kilogram of corn converted into spirits (marginal utility of spirits or, more properly, of corn used for making spirits) is a diminishing function of the quantity of corn used in this way, and consequently be expressed by $f(x)$. Then the solution of this problem consists simply of equating these two functional values:

$$F(a - x) = f(x) \qquad (8.17)$$

Or one could conceive the marginal utility of spirits directly as a function of the quantity of spirits produced. If we suppose that from m kilograms of corn one obtains one litre of spirits, the supply of spirits produced amounts to $\frac{x}{m}$ litres. The enjoyment of the last litre of spirits produced must then be expressed by $f_1\left(\frac{x}{m}\right)$, where f_1 represents a new function. But now, when equilibrium has occurred, this enjoyment must be as great as the enjoyment of the last m units of the remaining corn, or, which is the same, the marginal utility of spirits (enjoyment of one litre of spirits) must be m-times as great as the marginal utility of corn (enjoyment of one kilogram of corn). We therefore write

$$mF\left(a - x\right) = f_1\left(\frac{x}{m}\right)$$

and the problem would be solved – if one knew the forms of the functions $F\left(\right)$ and $f\left(\right)$ or $f_1\left(\right)$, and could replace them by exact mathematical expressions. Then it would only remain to solve the first or the second of the above equations for x, which would be a purely mathematical task. Our colonist solves the same problem by the experimental method, without having heard anything of this theory. When he has produced too little spirits, he distills some more; if he has produced too much, so that the remaining supply of corn is insufficient for his purposes, he will take particular note of this experience for the next year.

But even without knowing the exact forms of the functions, from these equations one can draw an important conclusion, which can, of course, also be easily arrived at without using any symbols. For one could also conceive the whole utility or value in use of the remaining supply of corn or of the quantity of corn converted into spirit as function of the quantities in question – functions which, of course, grow with the variable quantities, but more slowly than these. If we express them by $\phi\left(a - x\right)$ and $\psi\left(x\right)$, the marginal utilities $F\left(a - x\right)$ and $f\left(x\right)$ are, as we have already shown, their differential coefficients, the former with respect to $\left(a - x\right)$, the latter with respect to x.

If one sets oneself the task of determining x in such a way that

$$\phi\left(a - x\right) + \psi\left(x\right)$$

becomes a maximum, this problem can, as is known, be solved by making the differential coefficient of the sum with respect to x equal to zero. One consequently has

$$\frac{d}{dx}\phi\left(a-x\right)+\frac{d}{dx}\psi\left(x\right)=0$$

or, since

$$\frac{d}{dx}\phi\left(a-x\right)=-\frac{d}{d\left(a-x\right)}\phi\left(a-x\right)=-F\left(a-x\right)$$

and

$$\frac{d}{dx}\psi\left(x\right)=f\left(x\right)$$

$$F\left(a-x\right)=f\left(x\right)$$

which is the same equation as the one found at the beginning.

In other words, the solution of our original problem forms at the same time the solution of the problem of distributing the supply of corn between its two uses in such a way that the greatest possible total utility or total enjoyment arises from it

This, however, is self-evident; for the purpose of the production of spirits was just to obtain from one part of the supply of corn a higher enjoyment than was obtainable by its direct consumption; and the production will be continued as long as a further gain of utility is obtainable, that is to say, until the greatest possible utility is attained.

Beyond this, almost nothing, as was said before, is known *a priori* about the behaviour of the functions $\phi\left(\right)$ and $\psi\left(\right)$ or $F\left(\right)$ and $f\left(\right)$. At the outset it is only certain that $\phi\left(\right)$ and $\psi\left(\right)$ grow with the variable quantities under the sign of the function, but more slowly than these, and when these disappear, they become zero themselves. From this it follows that their differential quotients $F\left(\right)$ and $f\left(\right)$ are *diminishing* functions. The *simplest* approximating formula which satisfies these conditions is the one in which z indicates any variable quantity:

$$\phi\left(z\right)=\alpha z-\beta z^{2}\qquad\psi\left(z\right)=\alpha'z-\beta'z^{2}$$

consequently

$$F\left(z\right)=\alpha-2\beta z\qquad f\left(z\right)=\alpha'-2\beta'z$$

where α and β, α' and β' respectively are positive constants, whose values must be determined for each case. If here, for example, β is very small compared with α, then at first $\phi(z)$ increases almost proportionally with z, but afterwards more and more slowly, reaching a maximum for $z = \frac{1}{2}\frac{\alpha}{\beta}$; after that it decreases, finally becoming zero and even negative. The same is true of $\psi(z)$, if one replaces α and β by α' and β' respectively.

$F(z)$ and $f(z)$, on the contrary, have for small values of z almost the constant values α and α'; if z increases, they always decrease; they become zero where $z = \frac{1}{2}\frac{\alpha}{\beta}$ and $z = \frac{1}{2}\frac{\alpha'}{\beta'}$ respectively; and beyond that they become negative.

In this there is nothing which is inconsistent with experience, for the total utility as well as the marginal utility of a quantity of goods can finally become 'negative', that is to say, can change into *disutility*, if the existing quantity becomes much too great. For example: water, manure, dross, sawdust, etc.

But what it does not show is whether so simple an approximating formula meets even one single case sufficiently *exactly* to be applicable. In most cases, this is even most improbable. Launhardt, however, has made the most extensive use in his work of precisely this formula, without really examining even once how far it corresponds to the facts. It is at least doubtful, therefore, whether the fine results and conclusions which, by the help of this approximating formula, he has found and printed in italics, have anything to do with reality.

Nevertheless, it will be possible to assert, according to the analogy of physical events, that, if it is only a question of variation *within certain narrower limits*, such an approximating formula can be substituted *within this sphere* for the exact form of the functions, whatever the nature of the latter may otherwise be.

If, for instance, in our example above it is quite certain in advance that the value of x sought must lie between two limits b and c, which are known to lie not too far apart, it will be possible *within these limits* to use without hesitation the approximating formulae; that is to say, instead of equation (8.17)

$$F(a - x) = f(x)$$

we write

$$\alpha - 2\beta(a - x) = \alpha' - 2\beta'x$$

In order to be able in this case to determine the constants α, β, α', β', it is necessary to know for at least two values of x which belong to this sphere, the corresponding four values of the function of the marginal utilities $F(a - x)$ and $f(x)$. If we suppose *that* for $x = b$ the marginal utility of corn is v and the marginal utility of the corn converted into spirits v', and that for $x = c$ their values are w and w' respectively, α, β, α', β' can easily be expressed by v, w, v' and w', and we obtain

$$x = \frac{(v - v')(a - c) - (w - w')(a - b)}{v - v' - (w - w')}$$

or

$$= a - \frac{c(v - v') - b(w - w')}{v - v' - (w - w')}$$

This expression is, as can be seen, homogeneous in relation to the magnitude of v, v', w and w' and of degree zero. In other words, the value of x remains unchanged, irrespective of the measure according to which the marginal utility is estimated; only for *both* kinds of commodities or uses in question this measure must be one and the same. This, of course, cannot be otherwise. The utility of a commodity is something *sui generis*; it can be measured neither in metres nor in kilograms; it is comparable only with itself or with the utility of other goods. ...

Exchange at Given Prices

If we now turn to exchange in its real sense, we can first deal with the simple case, where the proportion of exchange of two commodities – or, if we conceive one of them as the price commodity and the other as the commodity, the *price* of the latter – is already fixed in advance, as, for example, is approximately the case in the retail trade. The buyer of the commodity then provides himself with so much of it and disposes of so much of the price commodity – in a proportion of exchange which has been fixed by the seller – so that finally the proportion of the marginal utilities of both commodities for the intended consumption period just equals the price.

Let us suppose, for example, that he has at the beginning the quantity b of the price commodity, or b units, but is still without the commodity, and that he must give for one unit of the commodity p units of the price commodity. If we then express the marginal utility of the commodity by F () and the marginal utility of the price commodity by f (), we get

$$F\left(x\right) = p.f\left(b - y\right)$$

where x indicates the number of the acquired units of the commodity and y the number of units of the price commodity given in exchange. Moreover, we have here

$$y = p.x$$

so that the problem is solved as soon as the forms of the functions F () and f () are known. ...

Isolated Exchange

If for *both* the exchanging persons the marginal utility of one or other of the commodities in question, which we will call (A) and (B), is altered by the exchange, and consequently the price is not fixed in advance, then – supposing the exchange to be completely isolated, that is to say, supposing that other possibilities of obtaining the desired commodity do not exist – one cannot possibly speak of a fixed proportion of exchange which can be theoretically determined: the problem is *indeterminate*. Only this much is certain, that an exchange will take place wherever both contracting parties derive, or believe that they derive, advantage from it, and that it will continue as long as it promises a further gain of utility on both sides, be it ever so small. If we suppose in particular, as we also did in the previous cases, that it is a matter of continuous quantities, that is to say, of commodities which are optionally divisible and can also be consumed optional quantities, it can be asserted that the exchange will cease only at the point at which the proportion of the marginal utility of the one commodity to that of the other is equal *on both sides*. If this condition is not yet fulfilled there will always exist on *both* sides a reason for continuing the exchange. If after the exchange has taken place, in the estimation of the original possessor of (A) one unit of the commodity (B) is still equal in value to three units of the commodity (A), whilst the possessor of (B) estimates that this quantity is equal to only $2\frac{1}{2}$ units of the commodity (A), then both believe that they will obtain an increase if the second of the contracting parties gives to the former another or several units of the commodity (B) against, for example, $2\frac{3}{4}$ units each of the commodity (A). But this tells us neither in what proportion the previous exchange took place nor how great the quantities were, nor consequently in what average proportion both commodities finally change their possessors.

The mathematical manner of treatment reflects this fact clearly. Let us suppose that one possessor has a units of the commodity (A) but as yet no units of (B); and that the other possessor has no units of (A) but b units of (B). Let us further assume that the function of marginal utility of the commodity (A) is $F()$ for the former possessor and $J()$ for the latter, and that the corresponding functions of the commodity (B) are $J()$ and $j()$ respectively. Then the exchange is continued up to the point where

$$\frac{F\left(a-x\right)}{f\left(y\right)} = \frac{J\left(x\right)}{j\left(b-y\right)} \tag{8.18}$$

x and y denote here the number of the exchanged units of (A) and (B) respectively.

But we have here only a single equation between two unknown quantities. The problem is consequently indeterminate; it has an infinite number of solutions. It could even appear as if, for each value of x, a y belonging to it could be found, and vice versa. This, however, is not so, because, as can easily be seen, the limiting condition must be added, that each of the exchanging persons ought to exchange with profit or at least without loss. The possible solutions consequently lie between two limits (margin pairs of x and y), in which cases the one or the other of the contracting parties has no profit at all (but also no loss). To determine these limits, when the functions of marginal utility are given on both sides, is a problem of the integral calculus. Let us think of the planned exchange as split up into an infinite number of partial exchanges, so that each time infinitesimal quantities, dx and dy, are exchanged against each other. If, then, the original possessor of commodity (A) gains nothing when he gives dx of (A) in exchange for dy of (B), the ratio $\frac{F(a-x)}{f(y)}$ of the marginal utilities to him of (A) and (B) must be the inverse of

$\frac{dx}{dy}$. We therefore obtain each time

$$F\left(a - x\right) dx = f\left(y\right) dy$$

or, if we add up from zero to x and y on both sides,

$$\int_0^x F\left(a - x\right) dx = \int_0^y f\left(y\right) dy$$

in which case the upper limits must satisfy the integral of the equation (8.18).

Both these integrals, as can easily be seen, represent the possessor of (A), *the total utility* of the quantity of the commodity (A) given in exchange, and of the quantity of the commodity (B) taken in exchange, respectively. If, therefore, these functions of the total utility, now found by integration, are expressed by $\phi\left(\right)$ and $\psi\left(\right)$ respectively, we get

$$\phi\left(a\right) - \phi\left(a - x\right) = \psi\left(y\right)$$

By this equation, in combination with equation (8.18), the values in question of x and y can be determined.

In the same way, if the analogous functions in respect of the possessor of (B) are expressed by χ and ω, the other limit of the possible proportions of exchange is given by

$$\chi\left(x\right) = \omega\left(b\right) - \omega\left(b - y\right)$$

always in combination with (8.18). Between the limits thus determined, every proportion of exchange must be declared possible.

In order to make the foregoing a little clearer by an example, we may be allowed to make the simplifying assumption that for *both* the exchanging persons (which we will call A and B), the functions of marginal utility of the same commodity are *identical*, so that $J\left(\right)$ is identical with $F\left(\right)$ and $j\left(\right)$ with $f\left(\right)$, and their values depend *only* on the possessed or exchanged quantity of goods, not on the personal dispositions or other circumstances of A and B. Moreover, let us suppose that both functions of marginal utility can be replaced by approximating formulae of the first degree, $\alpha - 2\beta x$ and $\alpha' - 2\beta' y$, *and this over the whole sphere of the problem*, which, of course, as already mentioned, can only be the case under special circumstances. The equation (8.18) then turns into

$$\frac{\alpha - 2\beta (a - x)}{\alpha' - 2\beta' y} = \frac{\alpha - 2\beta x}{\alpha' - 2\beta' (b - y)}$$

and if here numerator is added to numerator and denominator to denominator, each of these fractions becomes

$$= \frac{\alpha - \beta a}{\alpha' - \beta' b} = \frac{F(a) + F(0)}{f(b) + f(0)}$$

The ratio of the marginal utilities of the two goods, when equilibrium has been attained, is therefore, under the above assumptions, constant, independently of the values of x and y concerned, and equal to the proportion of the *average* marginal utilities of the quantities possessed. In whatever proportion the commodities here change hands by a repeated exchange, the last exchange which leads to equilibrium will always take place in the same proportion.[1]

Suppose that A has 10 oxen and B has 100 sheep, and that the marginal utility of oxen is expressed by $200 - 10x$, and the marginal utility of sheep by $10 - 0.1y$. That is to say, in B's estimation, if he does not yet possess on ox, one ox is worth 200 (e.g. 200 *Marks*, if the value of 1 *Mark* is regarded as constant); for every ox which he takes in exchange, the value of an ox will seem to him 10 (10 *Marks*) less, etc. The same is true for A, so that he, if he still possesses all the 10 oxen, estimates the value of 1 ox as 100 *Marks* only, but for every ox which he gives in exchange he will increase that value by 10 *Marks*, etc. In an analogous way the same is true of the marginal utility function of the sheep. Properly speaking, we are dealing here with oxen in the same way as with sheep, namely as optionally divisible continuous quantities; so that it would be more correct to say that B estimates the first fraction, for example the first hundredth of an ox, as worth 2 *Marks,* the second hundredth as worth *1 Mark 90 Pfennig,* etc.

---

[1]This circumstance was put forward by Launhardt (p.37) as a general rule, but it is evidently only valid under the above simplifying assumptions, which are however, by no means general.

We therefore have here

$$\alpha = 200, \qquad 2\beta = 10, \qquad \alpha' = 10, \qquad 2\beta' = 0.1$$

When equilibrium has been attained, we necessarily get

$$\frac{200 - 10\,(10 - x)}{10 - 0.1y} = \frac{200 - 10x}{10 - 0.1\,(100 - y)}$$

or, written in a shorter way,

$$\frac{100 + 10x}{10 - 0.1y} = \frac{200 - 10x}{0.1y}, \quad \text{consequently,} \quad = \frac{30}{1}$$

as follows by the addition of numerator to numerator and denominator to denominator. The last fraction expresses the constant and on both sides equal proportion of the marginal utilities in case of equilibrium, and consequently also the proportion on which both commodities are *at last* always exchanged.

The above equation finally reduces itself, as can easily be found, to

$$10x + 3y = 200$$

This equation must always be fulfilled after the exchange has taken place, but otherwise, within the above-mentioned limits, all possible proportions of exchange can occur. In order to determine these limits, we put, as we have already ascertained, supposing that A exchanges without any profit,

$$\int_0^x (100 + 10x)\, dx = \int_0^y (10 - 0.1y)\, dy$$

or

$$100x + 5x^2 = 10y - \frac{y^2}{20}$$

But if B exchanges without profit,

$$\int_0^x (200 - 10x)\, dx = \int_0^y 0.1y\, dy$$

or

$$200x - 5x^2 = \frac{y^2}{20}$$

each time in conjunction with the equation

$$10x + 3y = 200$$

From these equations we obtain for the one limit

$$\begin{aligned} x &= 6\sqrt{5} - 10 \\ &= 3.42 \\ y &= 100 - 20\sqrt{5} \\ &= 55.28 \end{aligned}$$

and for the other limit

$$\begin{aligned} x &= 20 - 6\sqrt{10} \\ &= 1.03 \\ y &= 20\sqrt{10} \\ &= 63.24 \end{aligned}$$

The possible proportion of exchange will consequently be able to fluctuate between about 1 ox against 61 sheep and 3.4 oxen against only 55 sheep (or on an average 1 ox against about 16 sheep). In the first case B, and in the second A, will have exchanged without any profit (but also without loss).

As the proportion of marginal utility amounts in the end always to '1 ox worth 30 sheep' it could, for example, be supposed that both the contracting parties had from the beginning agreed to exchange in just this proportion. One would then have, beside the equation

$$10x + 3y = 200$$

which is always fulfilled, the equation

$$x = 30y$$

so that $x = 2$ and $y = 60$; that is to say, A gives 2 oxen to B and gets in return 60 sheep. It is easy to show that the gain of utility then becomes *the same* on both sides, namely 200 (*Marks*).[2]

---

[2]For A's total utility increases by

$$10y - \frac{y^2}{20} - 100x - 5x^2 = 200$$

and B's by

$$200x - 5x^2 - \frac{y^2}{20} = 200.$$

This characteristic feature also was noticed by Launhardt. It is valid, however, only under the above-made assumptions, which, as he asserts, are by no means 'to be regarded as approximately right', but at best permissible by way of example.

But if, for instance, B knows how to direct the proportions of exchange to his advantage, 3 oxen against only $56\frac{2}{3}$ sheep (on an average 1 ox against 19 sheep) might be given by A. But A might perhaps not be inclined to do this in a single exchange, for although at first he values 1 ox as equivalent to 10 sheep, this proportion of marginal utility would have risen to '1 ox worth 30 sheep' after the exchange, so that the transaction could appear to him as of doubtful use, though in reality it would bring him no loss according to our assumptions.

But supposing that he was first expected to exchange 1 ox for 13 sheep, then a second ox for $17\frac{2}{3}$ sheep, then $\frac{1}{2}$ ox for 11 sheep and finally another $\frac{1}{2}$ ox for 15 sheep, then there would remain for him *after* each exchange respectively a proportion of exchange between sheep and oxen of more than 1:13, 1:$17\frac{2}{3}$, 1:22, and finally of just 1:30, so that each single exchange would have to seem to him undoubtedly profitable, although he has in fact finally exchanged just 3 oxen for not quite 57 sheep.

In the case of isolated exchange, too, of course, a kind of maximum problem is solved, for each of the exchanging persons strives after the greatest possible profit and is inclined to continue the exchange until he can derive no further profit from it. But since the whole problem is indeterminate, one can speak of a definite solution only when new conditions are added.

Such a condition would be, for instance, to determine the quantities of goods which are to be exchanged in such a way that the gain of utility attained *by both the contracting parties together*, in other words, approximately the 'economic' profit, becomes the greatest possible one. It is self-evident that, if this aim is attained by the exchange which has taken place, the proportion of marginal utility of both commodities on each side must be the same and that consequently the equation (8.18) must be fulfilled, for otherwise the exchange could always, as we have seen, be continued with a gain of utility *on both sides*, so that the gain of utility already attained could not possibly be the greatest possible one. But this does not mean that the solution of this problem belongs to the *possible* solutions mentioned above.

The mathematical treatment of this problem is very simple; one has only to express that the sum of the gains of utility on both sides or, which is the same, the sum of the total utility attained on both sides

$$\phi(a - x) + \psi(y) + \chi(x) + \omega(b - y)$$

is to be as great as possible. Since x and y are here independent of each other, one must consequently have at the same time

$$\frac{d}{dx}[\phi(a - x) + \chi(x)] = 0$$

or, differently expressed,

$$F(a - x) = J(x)$$

and

$$\frac{d}{dy}[\psi(y) + \omega(b - y)] = 0 \text{ or } f(y) = j(b - y)$$

By this the equation (8.18) is obviously exactly fulfilled; but whether the pair of values of x and y, so determined, really lies within the limits of the possible exchange, has still to be decided. ...

Supply and Demand

... However, a more detailed examination shows that equality of supply and demand is indeed a *necessary*, but, at least from the theoretical point of view, not a *sufficient* condition for the equilibrium of the market, supposing the latter to be *stable* – if, that is to say, the proportion of exchange would automatically return to (approximately) the same position after an accidental shifting.

If, for instance, it is a matter of demand and supply of the commodity (A), it can generally be asserted that, if p increases, the demand for (A) always falls; if, on the contrary, p decreases, the demand for (A) will always increase. If we could now be certain that, on the contrary, the supply of (A), at least near the equilibrium price found ... would increase when the price rose, and would decrease when the price fell, then the stability of the equilibrium would obviously be secured; for in the case of an accidental deviation of the price upwards the supply would be greater than the demand; in the case of a deviation downwards, the demand would, on the contrary, exceed the supply;

in both cases the inequality of supply and demand would necessarily drive back the price to approximately the earlier position.

But we know in regard to the supply of (A) that this magnitude, multiplied by the price of (A), represents the demand for (B) $(Y = pX)$.

If now the demand for (A) decreases when the price of (A), expressed in terms of (B), rises, then the demand for (B) must for the same reason diminish when the price of (B), expressed in terms of (A), rises, and consequently increase if the price of (A), expressed in terms of (B), rises. If therefore we put the demand for (A) or $X' = \phi(p)$ and the demand for (B) or $Y = \psi(p)$, then $\phi(p)$ is consequently a decreasing function (when p increases); $\psi(p)$, on the other hand, is an increasing function of p. We therefore obtain for the supply of (A) or X the expression

$$X = \frac{1}{p}\psi(p)$$

which product, for different values of p, can under certain circumstances increase with increasing p but also decrease. If $\psi(p)$ increases more rapidly than p, this product increases; if $\psi(p)$, on the other hand, increases less rapidly than p, it decreases.

When the price rises, therefore, not only the demand but also the supply of the commodity in question can decrease. If, now, the demand decreases more *rapidly* than the supply (and therefore, on the contrary, increases more rapidly when the price falls), the stability of the equilibrium is, as can easily be seen, even in these circumstances still secured. But there is nothing to prevent $\frac{\psi(p)}{p}$ from decreasing or increasing even more rapidly than $\phi(p)$, near the value of p in question, since supply and demand of the same commodity proceed from different persons and are consequently totally independent of each other.

If this is the case, no real equilibrium of the price exists, but only a temporary equality of supply and demand; for as soon as the price moves even in the least degree upwards the demand will be greater than the supply and the price must consequently rise higher and higher, until the demand, decreasing, finally catches up with the decreasing supply once more. In the same way a small shift of the price downwards will cause the supply to exceed the demand, and leads therefore to lower and lower prices, until the demand, increasing, again catches up with the increasing supply.

In both cases equilibrium is finally reached, but the equilibrium price will in each case be a different one. Thus the further peculiarity arises, that not only one, but two *different* (stable) *states of equilibrium* of the market would theoretically be possible.

Walras, and Launhardt after him, have drawn supply and demand curves in hypothetical form. By this means the price is represented as abscissa of a right-angled system of co-ordinates, and the quantities of goods demanded or supplied as ordinates of the different curves. Mangoldt, by the way, in his *Grundriss der Volkswirtschaftslehre*, which was published in 1863, had already drawn similar curves, which, however, were eliminated by the editor of the later edition of his work.

I reproduce ... Launhardt's diagram, in which certainly, the peculiarity mentioned above does not appear. Here, for the sake of greater clarity, two of these curves are drawn beneath the axis of the abscissae. If p is zero, i.e. if the commodity (A) is to be had for nothing, everybody, and consequently the possessors of (B) also, will provide themselves with it until saturation is reached, but they will not desire an infinite quantity of it. The demand curve therefore cuts the axis of ordinates at a certain distance from zero. If p increases, the demand for (A) on the part of the possessors of (B) decreases, and at a certain price this demand becomes zero.

The demand curve for (B) would now follow a similar course if the abscissa represented, instead of the price of (A) expressed in terms of (B), the price of (B) expressed in terms of (A) – that is to say, if π were chosen as abscissa. But in that case the demand for the commodity (B) will only begin at a value of p different from zero. From then on the demand for (B) increases as p increases, but will never be able to exceed a certain magnitude, namely the quantity of (B) which would be desired if p were infinite and consequently $\frac{1}{p}$ were $= 0$, that is to say, if the commodity (B) could be had for nothing. The demand curve for (B) therefore approaches asymptotically a straight line which is drawn at this distance parallel to the axis of the abscissa. The two curves mentioned so far, by the way, are absolutely independent according

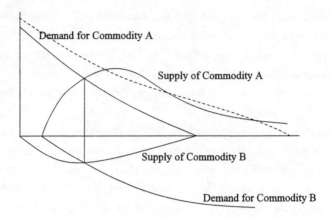

Figure 8.4: Multiple Equilibria

to our assumptions.

Each of the other two curves, on the contrary, is totally determined by the form of each of the previous curves. If the demand for (A) is given by the function $\phi(p)$, the supply of (B), as we have seen, is necessarily represented by $p.\phi(p)$; in the same way $\frac{1}{p}\psi(p)$ expresses the supply of (A), if $\psi(p)$ expresses the demand for (B).

A direct consequence of this is, that the point of intersection of the supply and demand curves of (A) must lie vertically above the point of intersection of the supply and demand curves of (B). Both points of intersection determine one and the same value of p, namely the equilibrium price.

As regards the supply curve of the commodity (A) in particular, this has, as can be seen, a highest point and approaches afterwards the axis of the abscissa asymptotically. But although it is quite independent of the form of the demand curve of *the same* commodity, its intersection point with the latter can lie just as well on the right side of the highest point as on its left side (as in the figure). These two positions of the intersection point correspond to our two above-mentioned cases of stable equilibrium of the price. But this does not prevent these two curves from being able to have *more* than one point, and if so at least three points of intersection in common, as, for example, is shown by the dotted line drawn in our figure.[3] If this is the case, the two extreme intersection points, as we can easily convince ourselves, determine prices of stable equilibrium. The middle intersection point, on the contrary, shows no real equilibrium of prices, as was mentioned above, but only a temporary equality of supply and demand.

---

[3]In this case, the curves of the commodity (B) also would, of course, intersect at three points, lying vertically under the points of intersection of the curves of commodity (A).

Bibliography

[1] Allen, R.G.D. and Bowley, A.L. (1935) *Family Expenditure: A Study of its Variation*. London: P.S. King and Son.

[2] Amano, A. (1968) Stability conditions in the pure theory of international trade: a rehabilitation of the Marshallian approach. *Quarterly Journal of Economics*, 82, pp. 326-339.

[3] Appleyard, D.R. and Ingram, J.C. (1979) A reconsideration of the additions to Mill's 'great chapter'. *History of Political Economy*, 11, pp. 459-476.

[4] Atkinson, A.B. and Stiglitz, J.E. (1980) *Lectures on Public Economics*. London: McGraw-Hill.

[5] Baumol, W. and Goldfeld, S.M. (1968) *Precursors in Mathematical Economics: An Anthology*. London: London School of Economics.

[6] Bhagwati, J. and Johnson, H.G. (1960) Notes on some controversies in the theory of international trade. *Economic Journal*, 70, pp. 74-93.

[7] Black, R.D.C. (ed.) (1977) *Papers and Correspondence of W.S. Jevons, Vols ii* and *iii*. London: Macmillan.

[8] Bowley, A.L. (1924) *The Mathematical Groundwork of Economics*. Oxford: The Clarendon Press.

[9] Buchanan, J.M. (1971) The backbending supply curve of labour: an example of doctrinal retrogression? *History of Political Economy*, 3, pp. 383-390.

[10] Cantillon, R. (1931) *Essai sur la Nature de Commerce en Général.* (translated and edited by H. Higgs). London: Dent.

[11] Chipman, J.S. (1965) A survey of the theory of international trade. *Econometrica*, 33, pp. 477-519.

[12] Cochrane, J.L. (1975) William Whewell's mathematical statements. *Manchester School*, 43, pp. 396-400.

[13] Collard, D. (1968) Introduction to J.E. Tozer, *Mathematical Investigations of the Effect of Machinery* (1838). Reprinted New York: Kelley.

[14] Cournot, A.A. (1927) *Researches into the Mathematical Principles of the Theory of Wealth.* Translated by N.T. Bacon and introduced by I. Fisher. London: Stechert-Hafner.

[15] Creedy, J. (1980) The early use of Lagrange multipliers in economics. *Economic Journal,* 90, pp. 371-376.

[16] Creedy, J. (1986a) *Edgeworth and the Development of Neoclassical Economics.* Oxford: Basil Blackwell.

[17] Creedy, J. (1986b) On the King-Davenant law of demand. *Scottish Journal of Political Economy,* 33, pp. 193-212.

[18] Creedy, J. (1989) Whewell's translation of J.S. Mill. *Scottish Journal of Political Economy*, 36, pp. 266-281.

[19] Creedy, J. (1990a) Marshall and International Trade. In *Centenary Essays on Alfred Marshall* (ed. by J.K. Whitaker), pp. 79-107. Cambridge: Cambridge University Press.

[20] Creedy, J. (1990b) Marshall and Edgeworth. *Scottish Journal of Political Economy,* 37, pp. 18-39.

[21] Creedy, J. (1991a) The role of stocks in supply and demand analysis: Wicksteed's problem. *Oxford Economic Papers,* 43, pp. 689-701.

[22] Creedy, J. (1991b) Consumers' surplus and International trade: Marshall's example. *The Manchester School*, LIX, pp. 295-304.

[23] Creedy, J. (1992a) Jevons's complex cases in the theory of exchange. *Journal of the History of Economic Thought*, 14, pp. 55-69.

[24] Creedy, J. (1992b) Cournot on trade between regions and the transition from partial to general equilibrium modelling. *History of Economics Review*, 18, pp. 10-19.

[25] Creedy, J. (1992c) *Demand and Exchange in Economic Analysis: A History from Cournot to Marshall*. Aldershot: Edward Elgar.

[26] Creedy, J. (1994a) Launhardt's model of exchange. *Journal of the History of Economic Thought*, 16, pp. 40-60.

[27] Creedy, J. (1994b) Exchange equilibria: bargaining, utilitarian and competitive solutions. *Australian Economic Papers*, 33, pp. 34-52.

[28] Creedy, J. (1996) *General Equilibrium and Welfare*. Aldershot: Edward Elgar.

[29] Creedy, J. and Martin, V. (1993) Multiple equilibria and hysteresis in simple exchange models. *Economic Modelling*, pp. 339-347.

[30] Creedy, J. and Martin, V. (1994) A model of the distribution of prices. *Oxford Bulletin of Economics and Statistics*, 56, pp. 67-76.

[31] Cunynghame, H. (1892) Some improvements in simple geometrical methods of treating exchange value, monopoly and rent. *Economic Journal*, 2, pp. 35-52.

[32] Cunynghame, H. (1903) The effect of export and import duties on price and production examined by the graphic method. *Economic Journal*, 13, pp. 313-323.

[33] Cunynghame, H. (1904) *A Geometrical Political Economy*. Oxford: The Clarendon Press.

[34] Edgeworth, F.Y. (1881) *Mathematical Psychics*. London: Kegan Paul.

[35] Edgeworth, F.Y. (1889) The Mathematical Theory of Political Economy. *Nature,* Sept., pp. 434-436.

[36] Edgeworth, F.Y. (1894) The pure theory of international values. *Economic Journal,* 4, pp. 35-50, 424-443, 606-638.

[37] Edgeworth, F.Y. (1905) Review of Cunynghame's *Geometrical Political Economy. Economic Journal,* 15, pp. 62-71.

[38] Edgeworth, F.Y. (1925) *Papers Relating to Political Economy.* London; Macmillan for the Royal Economic Society.

[39] Fraser, L.M. (1937) *Economic Thought and Language.* London: Macmillan.

[40] Hearn, W.E. (1863) *Plutology: or the Theory of the Effort to Satisfy Human Wants.* Melbourne: George Robertson.

[41] Henderson, J.P. (1985) The Whewell group of mathematical Economists. *Manchester School,* 53, pp. 404-431..

[42] Hicks, J.R. (1934) Leon Walras. *Econometrica,* 2, pp. 338-348.

[43] Hicks, J.R. (1984) *The Economics of John Hicks* (ed. by D. Helm). Oxford: Basil Blackwell

[44] Hutchison, T.W. (1950) Insularity and cosmopolitanism in economic ideas 1870-1914. *American Economic Association. Papers and Proceedings,* 45, pp. 1-16.

[45] Hutchison, T.W. (1953) *Review of Economic Doctrines 1870-1929.* Oxford: Oxford University Press.

[46] Jaffé, W. (1965) *Correspondence of Leon Walras and Related Papers.* 3 Vols. Amsterdam: North Holland.

[47] Jaffé, W. (1983) *Essays on Walras* (ed. by D.A. Walker). Cambridge: Cambridge University Press.

[48] Jenkin, F. (1870) *The graphic representation of the laws of supply and demand.* Reprinted in 1931 in LSE Reprints of Scarce Tracts, no.9. London: Longmans, Green.

[49] Jenkin, F. (1871) On the principles which regulate the incidence of taxes. Reprinted in *Readings in the Economics of Taxation* (ed. by R.A. Musgrave and C.S. Shaup), pp. 227-239. London: Allen and Unwin.

[50] Jevons, W.S. (1909) *The Principles of Science.* London: Macmillan.

[51] Jevons, W.S. (1957) *The Theory of Political Economy* (ed. by H.S. Jevons). New York: Augustus Kelley.

[52] Johnson, W.E. (1913) The pure theory of utility curves. *Economic Journal,* 23, pp. 483-513.

[53] Launhardt, W. (1993) *Mathematical Principles of Economics* (translated by H. Schmidt and edited by J. Creedy). Aldershot: Edward Elgar.

[54] Marshall, A. (1876) J.S. Mill's theory of value. Reprinted in *Memorials of Alfred Marshall* (ed. by A.C. Pigou), 1925. London; Macmillan.

[55] Marshall, A. (1923) *Money, Credit and Commerce.* London; Macmillan.

[56] Marshall, A. (1961) *Principles of Economics* (Variorum edition). London: Macmillan.

[57] Marshall A. (1975) *Early Economic Writings.* 2 Vols. (ed. by J.K. Whitaker). London: Macmillan.

[58] Marshall, M. and M.P. (1879) *Economics of Industry.* London: Macmillan.

[59] Meade, J.E. (1952) *A Geometry of International Trade.* London: Allen and Unwin.

[60] Mill, J.S. (1844) *Essays on Some Unsettled Questions of Political Economy*. London: Parker.

[61] Mill, J.S. (1920) *Principles of Political Economy* (ed. by W.J. Ashley). London: Longmans, Green.

[62] O'Brien, D.P. (1975) *The Classical Economists*. Oxford; Oxford University Press.

[63] O'Brien, D.P. (1993) *Thomas Joplin and Classical Macroeconomics*. Aldershot: Edward Elgar.

[64] Pennington, J. (1840) Letter to Kirkman Finlay Esq. Reprinted in *Economic Writings of James Pennington* (ed. by R.S. Sayers, 1963). London: London School of Economics.

[65] Phelps Brown, E.H. (1936) *The Framework of The Pricing System*. Oxford: Oxford University Press.

[66] Pigou, A.C. (ed.) (1925) *Memorials of Alfred Marshall*. London: Macmillan.

[67] Robbins, L.C. (1958) *Robert Torrens and the Evolution of Classical Economics*. London: Macmillan.

[68] Robbins, L.C. (1930) On the elasticity of demand for income in terms of effort. *Economica*, 10, pp. 123-129.

[69] Samuelson, P.A. (1948) *Foundations of Economic Analysis*. Cambridge, MA: Harvard University Press.

[70] Samuelson, P.A. (1952) Special price equilibrium and linear programming. Reprinted in *The Collected Scientific Papers of Paul A. Samuelson, 2* (ed. by J.E. Stiglitz), pp. 925-945. Cambridge, MA: The MIT Press. (1966).

[71] Schumpeter, J.A. (1954) *History of Economic Analysis*. London: Allen and Unwin.

[72] Shapley, L.S. and Shubik, M. (1977) An example of a trading economy with three competitive equilibria. *Journal of Political Economy*, 85, pp. 873-875.

[73] Stigler, G.J. (1965) *Essays in the History of Economics*. Chicago: University of Chicago Press.

[74] Theocharis, R. (1961) *Early Developments in Mathematical Economics*. London: Macmillan.

[75] Todhunter, I. (1876) *William Whewell. An Account of his Writings, with Selections from his Correspondence*. London: Macmillan.

[76] Turgot, A.R.J. (1973) In *Precursors of Adam Smith 1750-1775* (ed. by R.L. Meek), pp. 77-100. London: Dent.

[77] Van Daal, J. and Jolink, A. (1993) *The Equilibrium Economics of Leon Walras*. London: Routledge.

[78] Vázquez, A. (1995) Marshall and the mathematization of economics. *Journal of the History of Economic Thought,* 17, pp. 247-265.

[79] Vázquez, A. (1997) The awareness of Cournot's *Recherches* among early British economists. *Research in the History of Economic Thouht and Methodology*, 15, pp. 115-137.

[80] Vickrey, W.S. (1964) *Microstatics*. New York: Harcourt Brace.

[81] Viner, J. (1955) *Studies in the Theory of International Trade*. London: Allen and Unwin.

[82] Viner, J. (1958) *The Long View and the Short*. Glencoe: Free Press.

[83] Walras, L. (1954) *Elements of Pure Economics* (translated by W. Jaffé). London: George Allen and Unwin.

[84] Weintraub, E.R. (1985) *General Equilibrium Analysis*. Cambridge: Cambridge University Press.

[85] Whewell, W. (1850) Mathematical exposition of some doctrines of political Economy – Second Memoir. Reprinted (1968) in *On the Mathematical Exposition of Some Doctrines of Political Economy*. London: Gregg International Publishers.

[86] Wicksell, K. (1934) *Lectures on Political Economy* (translated by E. Classen and edited by L. Robbins). London: Routledge.

[87] Wicksell, K. (1954) *Value, Capital and Rent* (translated by S.H. Frowein). London: Allen and Unwin.

[88] Wicksteed, P.H. (1933) *The Common Sense of Political Economy* (ed. by L. Robbins). London: Routledge.

Index